THE FRIENDSHIP BOOK

of Francis Gay

D. C. THOMSON & CO., LTD.
London Glasgow Manchester Dundee

ISBN 0 85116 433 1

A Thought
For Each Day
In 1989

*Don't wait till you've a garden
To grow life's favourite flowers.
True friendships blossom,
Not in soil,
But happy, well spent hours.*

Anne Kreer.

JANUARY

SUNDAY—JANUARY 1.

TO the only wise God our Saviour, be glory and majesty, dominion and power, both now and ever. Amen.
Jude 25.

MONDAY—JANUARY 2.

RECENTLY the Lady of the House brought home from one of her shopping expeditions a new battery for our torch which, the wrapper claimed, was exceptionally long-lasting.

Well, we shall have to wait and see, but I don't suppose it can ever compete with the famous gold lamp designed by the sculptor Callimachus over 2300 years ago, and which used to stand at the Acropolis in Athens. Once filled with oil, it was said that it would burn for a whole year.

There are various things which can burn for us for many months if we will let them, and they will lighten our whole life — faith, hope and love, for example.

A happy New Year to every reader!

TUESDAY—JANUARY 3.

I RECENTLY came across two quite separate passages from different sources which seem to say much the same thing — a very important thing, too:

"The real international language is not Esperanto, but love."

"Kindness is a language which the dumb can speak and the deaf can hear and understand."

THE FRIENDSHIP BOOK

ICICLES

SOMETIMES short, sometimes long,
Often thick, often strong,
Dripping in the wintry sun,
Melting slowly, one by one,
Till, upon a sunny day,
All of them have gone away.

Troubles large, troubles small,
Come to each, come to all.
Like icicles on roof and tree,
So they visit you and me;
Their fingers with their icy grip,
Would seize the mind — to shatter it.

Yet icicles can never stay,
With the sun they pass away,
Dripping, dripping they become
Smaller, shorter till just one
Melts completely in the heat —
A pool of water at your feet.
So troubles, where God's love doth shine,
Melt away in His good time.

Margaret H. Dixon.

THE vicar had been in hospital for several weeks undergoing routine surgery and at last he was able to ask his churchwardens to let his parishioners know he was on the road to recovery.

The next day he was startled to find the following announcement on the church notice board:

"God is good. The vicar is better."

FRIDAY—JANUARY 6.

TWELFTH NIGHT is no longer celebrated as such, in fact it is usually the day when Christmas trees and decorations are taken down and put away until next year.

But even after the calendar was changed in 1752, celebrations continued on that day until the middle of the 19th century, for it was called Old Christmas Eve. There were big family gatherings with food and the wassail bowl of hot spiced ale and roasted apples. Afterwards they would go from house to house singing a wassailing carol.

Many country people believed that January 6th was the real anniversary of Christ's birth and claimed that certain shrubs blossomed on that day and that bees came buzzing from their hives at midnight. One of the loveliest beliefs, though, was that the cows were to be found on their knees at midnight with tears streaming from their eyes, as they commemorated the birth of the Saviour.

SATURDAY—JANUARY 7.

HABIT is hard to conquer. Remove the first letter, and it doesn't change *a bit*. Remove the second and you still have a *bit* left. Remove the third, and the whole of *it* remains. But now remove the fourth, and you have conquered the habit. Which goes to prove that if you want to get rid of a habit, you must dispose of it altogether — you can't do it in bits!

SUNDAY—JANUARY 8.

BUT The word of the Lord endureth for ever. And this is the word which by the gospel is preached unto you.

Peter I 1,25.

WINTER TRACERY

THE FRIENDSHIP BOOK

THINK the Winter will never end? Miriam Eker's poem "Very Soon" reminds us of the joys around the corner:

> Soon the gardening will call
> The Master of the House!
> Soon there'll be a cleaning
> From his energetic spouse!
> Soon the sun will show its face,
> A little more each day —
> Soon the fireside will pall,
> With Winter pushed away!
> Soon we'll venture out of doors,
> In lighter clothes appear;
> Soon the world will be reborn —
> For Spring is drawing near!

MRS STENHOUSE was delighted when she heard that she had been chosen as one of the tenants of a newly-built block of homes for old folk. She was telling us about her good fortune when we met her in the baker's. The family had all rallied round, giving her new curtains, an armchair and pot plants.

"I'm moving tomorrow," said this cheerful 80-year-old. "When I'm settled in you'll all be sure to come to see me, won't you?"

Just a week later we learned that she had passed away peacefully in her sleep. Some of us were saying how sad it was she had had her new home for so short a time, but old Peter Allan, who had been one of Mrs Stenhouse's neighbours, said simply, "I think it was splendid she *did* have it."

I'm sure he was right.

THE FRIENDSHIP BOOK

"IF a thing's worth doing, it's worth doing well."
Our teacher tried hard to guide us in the way we should go, using such time-honoured sayings as counsels of perfection. This one was a favourite of hers. She would illustrate it with the story of Josiah Wedgwood and how he walked through his factory closely examining every item. Any object which did not reach his high standards was promptly destroyed with the words, "That will not do for Josiah Wedgwood!"

It was a splendid example, but wasn't it rather a waste? Nowadays they would sell the rejected pieces as "seconds", which many would be happy to possess.

There is another side to the picture, too. Nowadays, many people have taken up pottery as a satisfying and relaxing hobby. They are never likely to produce a Wedgwood masterpiece, but their work still gives them infinite pleasure. Does this perhaps suggest that the old adage should be re-written?

"If a thing's worth doing, it's worth doing badly."

KAGAWA of Japan was one of the modern day saints. As a young man he was wealthy, but when he became a Christian he gave up the comforts and pleasures of his life to live in the Shinkowa slums of Japan. Here he mixed with the lowest of the low — criminals of all kinds, shunned and despised for their poverty and degradation.

Kagawa lived with them in their filthy alleyways so that he could help them. He dedicated his life to them and by his unselfish example enabled many to rise again from the mire of despair.

CONTEMPLATIONS

A

FRIDAY—JANUARY 13.

MY friend Andrew Miller lives in a house 500 feet up near the top of a hill. Quite often in Winter, when I go to see him, I walk into sunshine, while below I have been snuffling and sneezing in the fog. I tell him what a lucky man he is.

But in Summer, when Andrew comes to see us and we perhaps are having tea in the garden, he will say, "It was chilly up at our place today — you're protected from the cold wind down here. You're lucky!"

We're all lucky in some things, aren't we?

SATURDAY—JANUARY 14.

"KEEP your eyes open before marriage, and half shut after."

I came across this maxim recently and my first reaction was to smile. However, once I'd thought about it I realised its wisdom. A marriage requires tolerance on both sides and sometimes this will mean closing our eyes to our partner's faults. In fact, most of our relationships would blossom if we did this more often!

Mother Julian of Norwich had this to say on the same theme more than 500 years ago: "To love a human being means to accept him, to love him as he is. If you wait to love him until he has got rid of his faults, until he is different, you are only loving an idea."

SUNDAY—JANUARY 15.

THIS then is the message which we have heard of him, and declare unto you, that God is light, and in him is no darkness at all.

John I 1,5.

B

THE FRIENDSHIP BOOK

IN one of his books, Quentin Reynolds, an American journalist and BBC commentator during the last war, tells of seeing a shabbily uniformed commissionaire standing at the doorway of a building in London. As he watched, an Army officer passed and saluted the old man. Puzzled, Reynolds waited and saw a high-ranking Air Force officer go by and also salute. He was followed by a general who did exactly the same.

Mystified, Reynolds crossed the road to take a closer look at the commissionaire whom everybody was saluting. On the man's tunic he could see the dark red ribbon of the Victoria Cross, the highest award for gallantry.

He explains that, when anyone is wearing the VC, even the highest ranking officers in any of the Services must salute it in recognition and gratitude for the bravery of the wearer.

An excellent tradition. Long may it continue!

AVE VERUM CORPUS is one of the loveliest of Mozart's pieces of music and has given pleasure to many. Yet it probably gave even more pleasure to the person for whom it was written.

Mozart's wife Constanze was in delicate health at the time and went to the spa town of Baden to take the cure. She stayed there with a choirmaster and his family who looked after her and treated her with great kindness.

It is believed that Mozart then composed this motet and gave it to his friend as a token of his gratitude. Surely no gift could be more appreciated by a lover of music!

—

THE FRIENDSHIP BOOK

I CAME across the following words in the January issue of a church magazine, and although they were intended as a "Thought for the New Year," they seemed equally appropriate for any fresh start —

"You can't change the past, but you can ruin a perfectly good present by worrying about the future."

I COULDN'T help overhearing the conversation of two little boys walking over the level-crossing of an electric railway the other day.

"I know these rails I'm stepping over aren't live," said the first one, "but I always avoid standing on them — just in case!"

"Oh," said the second, "that's funny! I always walk on them deliberately just to prove that they're not!"

The latter's approach to life may not be scientific — indeed, on other occasions it could possibly be described as foolhardy — but there's certainly no doubting that his outlook is full of faith and optimism!

THERE is something round the corner,
Might be good or might be bad,
Might be strange or quite exciting,
Or maybe something quite delighting,
It even could be sad.
For Life is an adventure,
We don't know what's in store;
Be we seven years or seventy,
There is something round the door.
                                   D. J. Morris.

THE young man looked down nervously at the little chapel's congregation. He had spent hours writing, rehearsing and memorising his sermon. Just as his tutor, the Rev. Richard Cecil, minister of Chipping Ongar, Essex, required him to do.

Now, faced with the expectant listeners, the young candidate for the London Missionary Society could not remember a word!

"Friends," he faltered at last, "I have forgotten what I had to say."

He fled from the pulpit and out of the chapel.

What a calamity! It was his second attempt at entering the Missionary Society, for he had already been turned down because of his tutor's report. What would happen now after all his studying, hard work and sacrifices?

He was too nervous even to preach to a small congregation . . .

Years later, that same man, David Livingstone, faced unknown dangers, diseases and peril in his explorations across Africa. He lectured to thousands of learned men and women during his furloughs in Britain.

If Livingstone had let that small, but, to him, momentous, preaching failure influence his life he would never have become the great Christian missionary and explorer he did. Instead, he put that day behind him, tried again, and won through.

AND he said unto them, Go ye into all the world, and preach the gospel to every creature.

Mark 16,15.

NATURE'S GLORY

THE FRIENDSHIP BOOK

THE Lady of the House found this verse in an old book:

> *If your lips would keep from slips*
> *Five things observe with care:*
> *Of whom you speak, to whom you speak,*
> *And how and when and where.*
> *If you your ears would save from jeers,*
> *These things keep meekly hid:*
> *Myself and I, and mine and my,*
> *And how I do and did.*

A FRIEND of ours who is an English teacher was once asked to fill in for an absent history master. He is interested in the subject but, as he freely admits, he is not very good at remembering dates. He thought he had better admit this to his new class at the outset. They were very sympathetic; indeed, at the end of term, they brought him a present — a box of dates!

TONIGHT all over the world, Scots will be holding Burns Suppers with the piping-in of the haggis and other ceremonies to commemorate the birthday of Robert Burns.

For people of all nationalities it would be a good idea to use today, before a meal, Burns's famous " Selkirk Grace ":

> *Some hae meat that canna eat,*
> *And some would eat that want it;*
> *But we hae meat, and we can eat,*
> *Sae let the Lord be thankit.*

THE FRIENDSHIP BOOK

AT the beginning of another New Year, this poem by Margaret H. Dixon is particularly apt:

If New Year wishes could come true,
How many things I'd like to do:
Fly to far-off distant places,
Watch the smiles on dark brown faces,
Climb the steeps of each tall mountain,
Quench my thirst within a fountain,
Whose sparkling bubbles curl and twist,
Shot through with purest amethyst;
But these are dreams that may not be
Worked out into reality.
Yet, there are lovely things that may
Fill with deep joy our every day:
Laughter that's innocent and clear,
Carols to greet the new-born year,
The scent of grasses after rain,
And honeysuckle in the lane,
The taste of muffins, warm for tea,
The calm, sweet, dear serenity
Of being loved and loving, too,
All of God's world, my friend — and you.

I EXPECT we have all known people getting on in years who nonetheless manage to preserve a vigorous and youthful outlook. If asked, I imagine most of them would have their own individual secret.

Compton Mackenzie, the well-known author, was once asked, late in life, for his secret. He replied, "Curiosity, zest, memory, a perpetual search for experience, a perpetual delight in people, books, trees, flowers, music." These, he said, kept him young and lively — surely a recipe worth following.

THE FRIENDSHIP BOOK

A BUSINESS acquaintance often describes himself as an "optimistic pessimist", meaning that though he hopes for the best, he is quite prepared to face the worst, too. Perhaps the key word in his statement is "hope". Optimism is founded on hope.

"Hope and patience are two sovereign remedies for all; the surest reposals, the softest cushion to lean upon in adversity". So wrote Robert Burton, the 17th century scholar and author.

Probably he had not as much to dismay him in life as had Oliver Goldsmith, the author of "The Vicar of Wakefield". Yet Goldsmith wrote:

Hope like the glimmering taper's light
  Adorns and cheers the way
And still, as darker grows the night,
  Emits a brighter ray.

Perhaps the Victorian author Eliza Lynn Linton was right when she wrote: "One must have one of two things to get on in this life — buoyant cheerfulness that cannot be submerged and that always rises to the surface like a cork, or grim, dogged determination not to be conquered".

The famous Scot, the late Sir John Reith, first Director General of the BBC once stated, "I do not like crises, but I like the opportunities they provide".

Surely that is the best attitude of all to face any ups and downs in life?

BE ye therefore perfect, even as your Father which is in heaven is perfect.

Matthew 5,48.

THE FRIENDSHIP BOOK

WE all know what it's like when we get one of those days on which we wake up feeling the whole world is against us. Well, I have a friend who tackles this morning depression in a splendidly practical way. She raids her sweet jar, and searches her small garden for a few flowers, then off she goes visiting . . . and not just the old, or the crippled, but perhaps a young mother alone in the house with a sick or fractious child, or just feeling cut off from people generally. My friend shares her small gifts with them but above all, she listens to them and shares news and family gossip.

"It never fails, Francis," she assures me. "I start the day right down in the dumps, and end up feeling on top of the world."

She makes others feel on top of the world, too!

A MOTORIST who had lost his way stopped in a village and asked a local, "What is this place called?"

"Do you mean by those who have to live in the one-eyed hole?" came the reply. "Or by those who are merely enjoying its quaint and picturesque charms for a short spell?"

How little we sometimes appreciate the blessings and beauties which lie close at hand. I knew someone who lived in London and he once admitted that he had never bothered to go and see many of the sights which tourists flock to visit.

The Bible writer made a shrewd observation when he said, "The eyes of the fool are in the ends of the earth." There is so much close at hand which could bring us delight if only we were sensitive to it.

FEBRUARY

WEDNESDAY—FEBRUARY 1.

H ERE is a thought worth pondering. It's from the American writer, R. G. Granville:

If you don't want trouble, don't think it, and don't say it. Words are thoughts with a birth certificate. Once said, they are firmly recorded.

Let's be sure that the only thoughts we record are ones worth recording.

THURSDAY—FEBRUARY 2.

M ANY may be surprised to learn that Christmas — at any rate, the official ecclesiastical season — ends only today. In the past it was marked by special services and candlelit processions.

Talking of candles reminds me of a saying I once heard a speaker use at a school speech day. "Teachers," he said, "are like candles which light others by consuming themselves."

Not teachers alone either — parents, doctors, nurses, friends, writers, musicians, artists; the list is endless. Indeed it includes, or *ought* to include, us all.

Worth thinking about on this Candlemas Day.

FRIDAY—FEBRUARY 3.

I N one of Germany's schools of learning is a motto under the heading "Character". It reads:

When wealth is lost, nothing is lost;
When health is lost, something is lost;
When character is lost, all is lost.

I can't help thinking that anyone who can read, remember and act on that motto has made considerable progress in the art of life.

MY GARDEN

*M*Y *garden is a haven*
From a world of weary care.
There's always utter freedom
And sweet contentment there.

My garden is an ally;
It helps consistently.
When a problem takes me captive,
The garden sets me free.

My garden is a teacher
With qualities galore,
Providing many lessons
I'd be foolish to ignore.

My garden is a ruler
Requiring understanding;
Sometimes quiet and gentle,
Sometimes so demanding.

My garden is a gallery
Of infinite delight,
Displaying many pictures
That are classics in their right.

My garden's an oasis,
And it's wonderful to find
My little piece of Eden
Can bring such peace of mind.

J. M. Robertson.

AND the grace of our Lord was exceeding
abundant with faith and love which is in Christ
Jesus.   Timothy I 1,14.

HELPMATE

A working dog has no time to spare
With wayward sheep beneath his care,
So come on, master, don't be slow,
The sun is up and it's time to go!

THE FRIENDSHIP BOOK

I WAS more than a little surprised, one morning, to discover a moorhen building her nest.

Firstly, it was February and bitterly cold with no feeling of Spring in the air. Secondly, she was building in the middle of a village brook against the metal grid that holds back driftwood and other vegetation. It was exactly the same spot she had built her nest last year and I had watched then as she struggled to rebuild it after the flood water had swept it away.

So why did she choose this unsafe place again? I shall never know, of course, except that many birds are creatures of habit.

They are not the only ones. I wonder how many of us continue to do things in a certain way, just because we have always been accustomed to doing so — even when it isn't wise or sensible to do so.

THERE'S a verse in the Book of Deuteronomy which reads: "For only Og king of Bashan remained of the remnant of giants; behold his bedstead was a bedstead of iron . . . nine cubits was the length thereof, and four cubits the breadth of it, after the cubit of a man."

That is all that is said about King Og. Nothing more about him is recorded other than the fact that he was so big his bed was extraordinarily large.

Other kings have been remembered for finer things — Edward as the Peacemaker, Alfred as the Great, and Richard as the Lionheart. King Og is remembered only for the size of his bed!

For what will we be remembered? What will our memorial be? It's up to us, isn't it?

THE FRIENDSHIP BOOK

IT has long been the custom for Christians to give up something for Lent — perhaps their favourite foods or sweets, or some luxury.

I was interested, therefore, to see a rather thought-provoking Wayside Pulpit poster outside a local church. It read simply:

"WHAT ARE YOU *TAKING UP* FOR LENT?"

This is a rather different emphasis, isn't it? It reminds us that true self-sacrifice can mean doing something positive for others, taking on some new challenge or responsibility or piece of service.

IN his book "Harvest of the Years", the great naturalist, Luther Burbank, wrote, "I cannot pass a strange plant or a carpenter using a new tool without stopping to ask, 'What is this? How does it work?' I am almost 77, but I am as inquisitive as I was at eight."

Who can doubt that his enquiring mind was, in part at any rate, the secret of his ever-youthful spirit!

I remember reading an appropriate quote, although I don't recall who said it: "When we stop learning, we stop living."

SEVEN-YEAR-OLD Joan, our neighbour's daughter, had been off school for several days, as she was feeling poorly, and her four-year-old sister was asked by a friend how Joan was. She received this reply: "She's a lot better, Miss. She's been to see the doctor, and he's given her some medicine. But we can't play with her, 'cos on the bottle it says, 'Keep away from children'."

THE FRIENDSHIP BOOK

VISITORS to Wotton-under-Edge in the Cotswolds can see a plaque outside a house in Orchard Street. It states that there, in 1837, Isaac Pitman invented his system of shorthand.

Had he not been sacked from the denominational school where he taught, Isaac might never have become world-famous. It was at that point that he opened a private school in Wotton, and amongst the subjects he taught was the system of shorthand then in use.

So interested did he become in this time-saving method of writing that he compiled a small instruction book on the subject. The publisher to whom he submitted it suggested that Isaac would do better to invent a new shorthand.

"I had no intention of becoming a shorthand author," he later stated. "The ambition of appearing before the public in that capacity never entered my mind."

His work "Stenographic Sound-hand" experienced small sales at first, and also received much criticism. One Manchester reviewer called it a "mass of absurdity".

As we all know, the critics were wrong. Pitman's shorthand became universally accepted and the inventor was knighted. Had Isaac Pitman been deterred by hard work and later criticism, the business world today would be a very different place.

FOR whosoever shall do the will of my Father which is in heaven, the same is my brother, and sister, and mother.   Matthew 12, 50.

MONDAY—FEBRUARY 13.

THE Lady of the House and I enjoy our walks, even in the Winter, though I must admit that on a particularly chilly day recently we were glad to come across a little wayside tea-room where a log fire was burning cheerfully in the grate.

I was reminded of some words of Buckminster Fuller, an American engineer, architect and poet, who was once asked by his small daughter, as she watched logs burning, "What *is* fire, Daddy?"

He replied, "Fire is the sun unwinding from the tree's log. When the log fire spits sparks it is letting go a sunny day of long ago and doing it in a hurry."

I don't know whether the little girl understood his meaning — I think she might, because children have wonderful imaginations. But I think *I* understand, and on that cold Winter's day not only did the Lady of the House and I rejoice in the cheerful warmth, but we had a glimpse, too, of Summers past, and yet to come.

TUESDAY—FEBRUARY 14.

MARGARET RILEY wrote this verse which I have pinned up above my desk where it catches my eye every time I am about to postpone some less than pleasant task:

You tend to put off those tedious chores,
Like sewing on patches or polishing floors.
"I'll do it tomorrow," you quite often say,
Though it would be much quicker to do it today.
Some tasks are simple, like polishing shoes,
It's the boring ones that you really should choose,
Then on the morrow you can chuckle and say,
"Oh, thank goodness I did that job yesterday!"

THE FRIENDSHIP BOOK

"HAVE you noticed," a minister once asked his congregation, "that everyone wants to be a success?"

He went on, "Anyone with a little drive, imagination, persistence, opportunity and luck can be a success. Anyone can be a success when things go well. But learning to cope with life's disasters, even if you can't keep it up all the time — that's *real* success."

A VISITOR to America was amused to hear a radio weather forecaster solemnly announce, "Today's weather is quite unacceptable." I imagine though, that he and everyone else would have to accept it just the same!

True, there are some circumstances in life which can be altered for the better and we always ought to be willing to do our share to bring such changes about; but there are some things, too, that we just have to accept, and our willingness to do that can save us so much unhappiness.

I READ recently of an unknown artist who had painted a lovely landscape, and then just as he was finishing it, he made some blots on the sky! He knew he couldn't remove them without spoiling the entire scene. What could he do? He didn't tear his hair. He just took his pencil and added to each blot a beak and wings until they became birds!

It isn't a bad way of dealing with troubles. Turn them into birds, give them wings — and your troubles will fly away.

THE FRIENDSHIP BOOK

THE older you are the more you will appreciate these verses by J. M. Robertson, but younger folk would do well to heed them, too!:

> *I thought I knew the answers,*
>   *When I was 17,*
> *And simply couldn't wait to grace*
>   *The intellectual scene.*
>
> *I thought I knew the answers,*
>   *When I was 21,*
> *But found that all life's question marks*
>   *Had only just begun.*
>
> *I thought I knew the answers,*
>   *When I was 33,*
> *Yet soon discovered Fate had played*
>   *Some funny tricks on me.*
>
> *I thought I knew the answers,*
>   *But hastened to recall,*
> *As time went by, it seemed that I*
>   *Just didn't know 'em all.*
>
> *Now I'm 59, I think*
>   *It's fairly safe to say,*
> *Experience can help, but still*
>   *I'm learning every day.*

BLESSED are they that do his commandments, that they may have right to the tree of life, and may enter in through the gates into the city.

Revelation 22,14.

THE FRIENDSHIP BOOK

AN elderly friend of mine was recalling the things she remembered best about her childhood. The incident that stood out most clearly was one day when she had been dressing her dolls, and her smaller sister, aged about six, asked her what she was doing.

"That's a secret!" snapped the older girl, and turned her back. Behind her she heard her little sister say gently, "If you like, I'll help you."

It was only a small incident, but more than 60 years later, that older sister told me, "I have never forgotten that gentle reply. It has often kept me from losing my temper and being rude to people. I learned a great lesson that day."

ST FRANCIS OF ASSISI is usually remembered for his love of animals and most of us are familiar with pictures of him in his monk's habit, surrounded by animals and birds lying trustingly at his feet.

However, there is a legend about him which may not be so well known.

When he was a young man he was very wealthy, but he had no peace in his soul; nothing that money could buy brought him any satisfaction. One day, when he was riding outside the city he met a leper covered in sores. Normally he would have passed by at a distance, but something compelled him to get down from his horse and put his arms round the man. As he embraced him, the leper turned into the figure of Jesus.

It is said that the experience so changed him that he spent the rest of his life in a monastery, serving God, and that there he found the peace that he had been seeking.

THE FRIENDSHIP BOOK

TODAY is special for Guides. It is Thinking Day, when the girls think of their sisters in the worldwide movement. They send friendly greetings and thoughts to over seven million of their companions and join with them in spirit to celebrate with perhaps a party, a service of worship, or special ceremony. It is the birthday of both Lord *and* Lady Baden-Powell, and wreaths are laid in Westminster Abbey by members of the Scout and Guide Movements on their memorial.

While they are thinking of their sister-Guides, let us adults, too, think about this movement and the fine training its young members receive from devoted leaders the world over.

THE River Taff in Wales is spanned by a bridge which has stood for over 200 years. It was built by a man who had never built a bridge in his life until he was persuaded to span the river at Pontypridd. His first attempt, with several arches, was guaranteed for seven years, but collapsed in a flood after a short time. His second effort consisted of a single arch, but he had barely finished when it cracked in the middle and collapsed, too.

Undaunted, William Edwards began again, and this time he built one long high arch, 140 feet across, very thin at the top, but with three holes running through the haunches. He reckoned this would help the bridge to resist both wind and water — and time has proved him right.

The bridge — known as the Rainbow Arch — stands today as a monument to one man's perseverance.

LOOK!

THE FRIENDSHIP BOOK

"I'VE a thought for your 'Friendship Book', Francis," said the Lady of the House one evening when she returned home from a meeting.

The speaker had been talking about anxiety and how to deal with it. She had quoted from the writer, the late Dr Leslie Weatherhead. He recommended "shutting the door mentally on each day when it was over." Nothing, he explained, could be altered by then. "If it had been a good day — thank God. If it had been a bad day, then rejoice that it is over and that at least you have landed neither in hospital nor in jail!"

Sound advice indeed!

CHARLES KINGSLEY is probably best remembered for his lovely book, "The Water Babies". He also wrote many fine poems. This little one may not be great verse, but it's always been one of my favourites:

> *Do the work that's nearest*
> *Though it's dull at whiles,*
> *Helping, when we meet them,*
> *Lame dogs over stiles;*
> *See in every hedgerow*
> *Marks of angels' feet,*
> *Epics in every pebble*
> *Underneath our feet.*

FOR with God nothing shall be impossible.

Luke 1,37.

THE FRIENDSHIP BOOK

IT is interesting, sometimes amusing, and often very humbling to walk round a churchyard and read the curious epitaphs on old gravestones. I think one of the most unusual I have come across was in the little country churchyard of St Clement's near Truro. It is in memory of a certain Elizabeth Gay, "who after a service of 40 years, finding her strength diminished, with unparalleled disinterestedness, requested that her wages might be proportionately lessened."

I hope her employers had the sense to see what a "treasure" they had in Elizabeth and did nothing of the sort!

But how refreshing it is to reflect that there always were and no doubt still are, people who are more concerned with what they can give than what they can get. And, you know, they are the happy ones!

THE regulars on the morning bus to town were on nodding terms and would often exchange a comment on the weather. The British weather being what it is, more often than not those comments took the form of mild grumbles. All except for one cheery little woman, that is. No matter what the conditions, she always seemed to be able to find something good to say.

"It's a cold wind," everyone might be complaining, but then she'd get on the bus with a smiling face, saying, "It's nice and warm in the sun this morning!"

And you'd suddenly realise that what she'd said was true — it was simply a different way of looking at the same situation.

How often things might be a lot better if we would only change our point of view a little.

MARCH

I WONDER if you have in your garden any Lent lilies, yellow ladies or butter and milk? You probably have, whether you realise it or not, because these are some of the names given to the daffodil. Often, when the days are still cold, we are reminded of the coming of Spring when we see these glorious blooms.

Geoffrey Smith, the television gardener, once remarked that the daffodil wouldn't seem half as attractive if it were flaming scarlet or deep purple. Somehow the fresh, delicate colours breathe the very essence of Springtime.

"Spring comes with gentle feet," someone once wrote — and how that gentle arrival rejoices our hearts!

WHEN the National Theatre in London was opened, part of the ceremony entailed sending up a rocket. As it soared towards the sky, shedding its shower of colourful stars, the actor, the late Sir Ralph Richardson, exclaimed, "I love rockets — they are so unnecessary!"

What a dull world it would be if it consisted only of the necessary and the utilitarian! It is the little extras, the occasional extravagances, which add so much to life's enjoyment.

They don't need to cost much — certainly not as much as a rocket — and they can be quite small. I'll tell you another thing, too — they are even more enjoyable if shared with others.

THE FRIENDSHIP BOOK

MICHELANGELO was putting some finishing touches to one of his statues when a friend called. A few days later his friend called again, and when he saw the statue, commented that the sculptor couldn't have done much to it since he was there last.

Michelangelo raised an eyebrow and replied, "I have retouched this part and polished that. I have softened this feature and brought out this muscle. I have given more expression to this lip and more energy to that limb."

"Oh, yes," said his friend, "but all these are trifles."

"Perhaps so," replied Michelangelo, "but trifles make perfection — and perfection is no trifle."

TOMORROW is Mothering Sunday when we remember with gratitude all that our mothers have done for us. Here are some words from a lovely prayer by Dr Leslie Weatherhead, well suited to the occasion:

O God, we thank thee this day for all good mothers. For their care and patience and love in childhood's earliest days, for the prayers they offered, the counsel they gave, the example they set, we give thee thanks. And now, perhaps, their hearts are anxious for loved ones far away. Grant to them fortitude, serenity and grace. Comfort them in their loneliness and grant them light at eventide.

I AM Alpha and Omega, the beginning and the end, the first and the last.   Revelation 22,13.

THE FRIENDSHIP BOOK

I ADMIT it: I'm sometimes a puter-offer. I'll find excuses for not doing a job when I could quite easily be getting on with it.

When I act like this, the Lady of the House will look at me very sternly, and then, quietly, repeat this little verse:

> If there's a job you ought to do,
> Although you hate to do it,
> You'd better get it done at once —
> Before you live to rue it.
> And when it's done (you will agree),
> How very, very pleased you'll be.

It always works!

GRANDAD had recently come to live in the Martin household. "Yes, he's always around now," he'd overheard his daughter Jenny confide to a friend. It made him wonder, was he in the way? If only he could make himself useful, he thought, it would make all the difference. But how?

One afternoon, Brian, the youngest, came in from school, tearful after taking a tumble in the playground. His mother wasn't back from the shops, so it was Grandad who dealt with the scraped knees, the bump on the head, and comforted the little boy till his mother returned.

"Aren't we lucky," Jenny said thankfully to her little son, "to have Grandad always around?"

Those words again, he thought, but this time there was no mistaking the love and warmth in them. It seemed there was a special place for him, after all.

THE FRIENDSHIP BOOK

AS recently as 1974, an area to the north of Stoke-on-Trent was an eyesore covered with the slag heaps and marl pits that were the legacy of the pottery industry.

Gradually, the land was reclaimed, landscaped and beautified with lakes and trees. The pinnacle of success came when the site was chosen to house the National Garden Festival, and in the Summer of 1986 it became a unique exhibition for garden lovers.

When the Festival closed at the end of the season, the special displays went also, but fortunately much of the beauty remained for future generations to enjoy.

Isn't it true that there is nothing so ugly or unpromising, no situation so hopeless that we are unable to bring something good out of it? Whether it is a disappointment in life, an unfortunate mistake or a broken relationship, let's do all we can to improve it while there is still time.

PARISHIONERS can sometimes exercise very protective instincts towards their minister as this humorous story, dating from last century, illustrates.

The minister of St John's was called in to see a man who was very ill. Neither the man nor his wife was a member of St John's and as the minister was leaving the house, he paused at the door and asked the lady earnestly, "My good woman, why do you not go to church?"

"Oh, but we do, sir. We go to St Mark's."

"Then why in the world did you send for me? Why didn't you send for your own minister?"

"Oh, we wouldn't risk him," she replied. "My husband's trouble is infectious!"

FRIDAY—MARCH 10.

I AM sure you have often reminded yourself, as I have, of how much we owe to other people — not only to our families and friends, but to all those, known and unknown, who have provided the rich heritage we share through art, music, science, literature and so on.

I wonder if any of us could express that sense of indebtedness more movingly than the way it is put in an inscription at Dallas University? It reads:

"We have all warmed ourselves before fires we did not build, and drunk water from wells we did not dig."

SATURDAY—MARCH 11.

EVERYBODY knows the story of the Good Samaritan who came to the help of the traveller who had been beaten up by robbers, but do you know the little story of the two men who passed by on the other side?

One caught up with the other and they began to talk. They agreed that highway robbery was a terrible thing and something ought to be done about it, so they set up a committee for the Suppression of Brigandage which soon had branches all over Palestine. In no time at all, people were organising flag days to raise funds.

Well, that's just a joke of course, but there are always some people who see where help is needed and give it to the best of their ability, while others never get beyond saying that something ought to be done.

SUNDAY—MARCH 12.

SALVATION belongeth unto the Lord: and thy blessing is upon thy people.

Psalms 3,8.

THE FRIENDSHIP BOOK

WHAT wonderful things we can do if we have the will!

Mrs Iris Wilkins of Leigh, in Essex, desperately wished to take part in a sponsored walk to support an appeal for breast cancer screening. The mile-long course was round Southend Hospital.

Not very far, but 63-year-old Mrs Wilkins had steel hips and used crutches, never walking more than a few steps from the house to the car.

She was, however, determined to undertake the walk, and to get more strength in her arms, her son gave her weight-lifting exercises. On the big day she joined 60 other grans. Hospital staff stood by with a wheelchair but she bravely struggled on, without their help.

Not only did she finish the course, but she was also able to hand over £140 to the cause.

I hope I remember Iris Wilkins the next time I'm tempted to put off doing something worthwhile because it might be too difficult.

THE former master of that great liner, *Queen Elizabeth 2,* once described a strange happening.

Apparently, a few years ago, she was cruising in the Pacific, when one of the wireless operators picked up a message sent out over 40 years before from the liner *Queen Mary.*

I suppose scientists can explain how this can sometimes happen, but to me that message, coming from goodness knows where, after all those years, is just another reminder that we live in a wonderful and mysterious world, about which truly wise men and women never believe they know all the answers.

THE FRIENDSHIP BOOK

A GREAT deal of advice is handed out to people at the end of their working lives, but I think these "Ten Commandments of Retirement" take some beating.

1. View retirement as the beginning of a new life, not as the end of the road.
2. Keep physically fit and mentally alert. Set a daily routine (not too rigid) and stick to it.
3. Maintain your customary neat appearance.
4. Try not to get under people's feet, but be helpful and companionable.
5. Adjust to your new budget. Do not fight it or resent it; neither become a miser.
6. Tomorrow must always be the most important day in your retirement calendar.
7. Do not live in the past; you have not retired from the world.
8. Do all things in moderation.
9. Do things you never had time for. Beware of the rocking chair.
10. Do not interfere with others.

THURSDAY—MARCH 16.

M RS D. J. MORRIS of York frequently sends me a few of her thoughts in verse. I particularly like this one:

> *When I was worn and weary*
> *And so many depended on me,*
> *And life seemed dark and dreary*
> *Why, then, He befriended me;*
> *He sent His love to cheer me*
> *When the day was dark and dim*
> *And I felt His Presence near me*
> *When I depended on Him.*

THE FRIENDSHIP BOOK

WHERE would we be without our public libraries and their devoted staffs? Far more ignorant than at present, I imagine, and lacking much of the joy and contentment that good reading affords.

Sometimes, when I walk into a library and look along those colourful shelves, I think of the man who gave vast amounts of money to found many public libraries in Britain.

Andrew Carnegie, the Dunfermline-born industrialist who made a fortune in America, never forgot his roots or his early struggles. He placed a high value on education and had a great respect for books. That's why, when he was giving away a large share of his fortune, he made sure that much of it was used to establish free lending libraries wherever there was most need for them. What a lot of pleasure he has given many people over the years!

JACK PEARSON, a friend of mine who recently celebrated his 80th birthday, seems remarkably young in his attitude to life. To be honest, his legs are getting a bit wobbly these days, but he had this to say about growing old:

"Nobody ages merely by living a number of years — people grow old only by deserting their ideals. Years wrinkle the skin, but to give up enthusiasm wrinkles the soul."

BLESSED are the meek: for they shall inherit the earth.
                                                    Matthew 5,5.

MAKING A START

You couldn't call it vanity,
A lady must look nice;
Laying a good foundation
Is always sound advice.

THE FRIENDSHIP BOOK

C H. SPURGEON, well-known for his published sermons, also wrote some Family Recipes which are worth taking note of:

For Repairing "Jars" — Use mutual love mixed with readiness to forgive; general good temper is an admirable cement.

Preserving — Our tempers are best preserved by using as little of the vinegar of sarcasm as possible, our hearts by using an abundance of the oil of grace (never fails).

To Cure a Cold — Do all the good you can, love your neighbour as yourself.

Pickles — Those persons get into them most who meddle with other people's business.

Tart — Such replies, which some think smart, generally lead to soreness (and often sourness).

Fritters — Gossiping, late rising and laziness soon fritter away precious hours.

Sweets — The sweets of "doing good to others" will never cloy. The more of them the better, say I.

A UGUSTUS PUGIN, the early 19th century architect, is perhaps best known for his work in association with Sir Charles Barry in designing the Houses of Parliament on which he spent 25 years. He also designed cathedrals and churches all over the country and wrote eight books — all this in a very short life. After his death a contemporary said of him, "He died at the age of 40 but in that time produced 100 years' work!"

He was an outstanding example of the truth of the saying, "We live in deeds, not years."

D

THE FRIENDSHIP BOOK

THE poet Rodney Bennett wrote this charming poem for Springtime:

Little brown seed, round and sound,
Here I put you in the ground.

You can sleep a week or two,
Then — I'll tell you what to do:

You must grow some downward roots,
Then some tiny upward shoots.

From the green shoots' folded sheaves
Soon must come some healthy leaves.

When the leaves have time to grow
Next a bunch of buds must show.

Last of all, the buds must spread
Into blossoms white or red.

There, seed! Now I've done my best:
Please to grow and do the rest!

DID you know that according to a survey taken by the University of Denver, people who believe in God are likely to live longer?

At the end of the survey, the report concluded, "By promoting peace of mind, a deep faith reduces the chances of suffering from stress-related illnesses, including heart disease and mental disorder. The truly religious drink less, smoke less and are less violent".

It stands to reason, doesn't it?

A BEAUTIFUL legend tells how a monk found the crown of thorns which Jesus wore and placed it on the altar in his church on Good Friday.

On Easter morning, the monk went to the chapel to remove the relic which he now felt was out of keeping with the joy of Easter Day. However, when he opened the door the whole place was filled with a wonderful perfume. The early morning sunlight, streaming through an eastern window, fell on the altar where lay, not the crown of thorns, but a crown of blooms. The thorns had blossomed overnight into flowers, rare and sweet and lovely.

SATURDAY—MARCH 25.

T WO teenagers were holidaying in the Highlands. Climbing one day they met Donald the shepherd, on the top of a hill. It was misty so there was no view to be had and the boys thought they would have a joke at Donald's expense.

"Do you get a good view from here?" asked one.

"Oh, aye, you can see a long way," replied Donald.

"How far?"

"Oh, very, very far."

"As far as America?" asked one cheekily.

"Oh, farther than that," said Donald.

"Oh, really?"

"Yes, just you wait till the mists go away," said Donald, "and you'll be able to see the moon!"

SUNDAY—MARCH 26.

F OR I know that my redeemer liveth, and that he shall stand at the latter day upon the earth.

Job 19,25.

THE FRIENDSHIP BOOK

WILLIAM PENN, the famous Quaker, once said, "Frugality is good, if liberality be joined with it. The first is leaving off superfluous expenses, the last is bestowing them to the benefit of others that need. The first without the last begets covetousness; the last without the first begets prodigality."

Quaint language, perhaps, but the message is clear — be careful, but be generous, too.

"YOUR cat enjoys being stroked," I said to little Timothy as he gently brushed the bundle of fur that was Tibby resting contentedly on his lap. It was impossible to say which of them was receiving greater pleasure!

His young, psychology-trained mother beamed, "We can all do with some psychological stroking," she said.

"How do you mean?" I asked.

"Well, when you say to me, 'How are you today?' and I can see you are making a really genuine inquiry, I know that you sincerely care about me and it does me good. And when compliments are paid to us, we respond positively, we feel uplifted and better for them — just like Tibby!"

Then she showed me this quotation from George W. Childs:

"Do not keep the alabaster boxes of your love and tenderness sealed up until your friends are dead. Fill their lives with sweetness. Speak approving cheering words while their ears can hear them and while their hearts can be thrilled by them."

Like little Timothy, the giver receives just as much pleasure as the recipient!

ESCAPE

Gentle curves and jagged angles,
Azure skies and cobalt seas,
Only Nature's mighty canvas
Justice does to scenes like these.

WEDNESDAY—MARCH 29.

THE Lady of the House and I recently boarded a train to make quite a long journey. As we settled in our seats, the guard's voice came over the sound system, announcing details of the journey, the eating facilities offered, and the stops we would make. At the end he finished, slowly and gently, "And may the Blessing of Jesus Christ be with you all."

You will not be surprised to hear we found that one of the most pleasant and peaceful journeys we have ever made.

THURSDAY—MARCH 30.

ONE of my friends goes the same way to work every day. As he drives along he keeps an eye open for things of interest and beauty — a lovely garden, the morning sun shining on the distant hills, the pretty dresses worn by girls on their way to work, the fresh appearance of a restored building . . .

I don't know if he realises it, but he is following the advice of Charles Kingsley, who said: "Never lose an opportunity of seeing anything beautiful. Welcome it in every fair face, every fair sky, every fair flower, and thank Him for it, Who is the foundation of all loveliness".

FRIDAY—MARCH 31.

IN the foreword to his book "Laughter Unlimited", the humorist, Bennett Cerf, gives as one of his reasons for being a provider of fun, "Nobody yet has gotten into a serious fight while he was laughing!"

It reminds me of the familiar old saying, "Laugh, and the world laughs with you."

APRIL

SATURDAY—APRIL 1.

MOST of us have a picture of ourselves that we hope others see. There is an interesting story told of the beautiful actress, the late Diana Wynyard. She had treated herself to a Spring hat with an outsize red rose and, sitting at a restaurant table one day, waiting for a friend to arrive, she saw a woman enter wearing an identical hat.

Rather taken aback, but deciding to be bold, Diana merrily called out "Snap!" The other woman stared then, startled, hurried off to a far corner of the restaurant.

Puzzled, Diana took out her handbag mirror and surreptitiously looked at her reflection. Then she realised that she wasn't wearing her red-rose hat!

SUNDAY—APRIL 2.

AND God said, let there be light: and there was light.   Genesis 1,3.

MONDAY—APRIL 3.

I READ somewhere of a man who had lived all his life in a busy city, and then, when he retired, went to live in the country where he complained that he couldn't sleep because it was so quiet!

I suppose we get conditioned to noise in this busy world, but we miss a great deal if we don't train ourselves to make and appreciate times and places for silence.

The poet, Christina Rossetti, wrote of "Silence more musical than song". Let's make some provision to "hear" that music today!

THE FRIENDSHIP BOOK

IT was a glorious Spring morning — the birds were twittering and a blackbird was happily whistling as heartily as if his life depended on the amount of song he produced. The shrubs and trees were heavy with fragrant blossom.

"I'm always terribly sorry for blind people, but especially at this time of year. They miss so much," an acquaintance remarked, sighing.

I agreed, but after leaving her, reflected that many blind people seem to know how to enjoy the countryside better than some of us who can see.

A few years ago, the vice-chairman of the Yorkshire Dale Society, Ken Willson, contacted a few other keen fellow-members to arrange walking outings for blind people. They became more and more ambitious and even decided to venture underground. Expert pot-holers rallied round and visits were arranged to local caves. The excursions were a great success, with the explorers reaching caverns that might have daunted sighted people.

Many of the blind — and those suffering from other handicaps, too — are an inspiration. They may miss seeing many things, but their inner eyes and adventurous spirit often enable them to get the most out of life.

I GOT up early one morning and rushed right into the day,
I had so much to accomplish that I didn't have time to pray.
Problems tumbled about me, and heavier became each task.
"Why doesn't God help me?" I wondered, and He answered: "You didn't ask."

THE FRIENDSHIP BOOK

IN the year 1838, Florence Nightingale was 18. The daughter of a privileged family, she was slim and tall, with wavy chestnut hair. She was sure to receive a flood of marriage proposals after her "coming out" ball. But in this young woman's heart there burned a restless urge to seek something more than the whirl of gaiety in which she lived. She was intelligent, with an eager, inquiring mind, and the conviction that she had been born to help others.

It took years of argument in the face of opposition from her family before she was able to begin training for the work she knew she was meant to do. In the end, as we all know, she succeeded and became the most famous nurse the world has ever known.

The will to succeed — a sense of mission — of course she had these. More than that, though, she had God on her side. The wonderful thing is that He is on our side, too, if we want Him.

FRIDAY—APRIL 7.

THESE definitions of grades of giving were made many years ago, but they are still as true today:

The "tip" level — my small change for God.
The "entertainment" level — I pay when I go.
The "emotional" level — I give when I feel like it.
The "good intention" level — I'll give more when I've got more to spare and provided it won't interfere with anything else.
The "Christian" level — I give as I have been given, systematically and sacrificially, gladly and ungrudgingly.

To give with a truly loving heart is one of the most beautiful things we can do.

THE FRIENDSHIP BOOK

I READ an article recently in which the writer said that there are about 90,000 people in Scotland who speak Gaelic, and that it is also spoken in some unexpected places such as Nova Scotia.

What intrigued me most, though, was that apparently there is no Gaelic word for "bored". Now, I can't help feeling it would be a good idea if other languages didn't have such a word, either!

Still, we can all make an effort never to use it. If Gaelic speakers can manage without it, so can everyone else!

AND on the seventh day God ended his work which he had made; and he rested on the seventh day from all his work which he had made.

Genesis 2,2.

WHAT a pity that when we do our Spring-cleaning, we don't also Spring-clean our *minds*!

We wouldn't dream of hoarding rubbish and old junk in our homes yet, year after year, we allow our heads to be lumbered with the same old prejudices, fears, worries and grievances.

Some of these were planted years ago; others are second hand, adopted to keep up with friends or fashion.

Some are harmless, but others, if we are honest, spring from bias, envy, pride, bitterness. Let's throw them out this Spring! Then we can fill the space they have left with positive thoughts of hope, faith, enthusiasm and love.

THE FRIENDSHIP BOOK

A GROUP of missionary doctors in Thailand were finding out the hard way how to deal with local people employed at the hospital where they worked. They were advised never to rebuke a Thai employee in front of anyone else, as it would cause unbearable loss of face.

One doctor protested, "That's all very well, but supposing one of the nursing aides has made such a mess of a job that I feel she must be rebuked?"

He was told, "Speak calmly and tell her that she has done the job very nicely, but that if she wants to make it perfect, then next time she must do this, that or the other."

It was very difficult for British missionaries, accustomed to speaking their minds, to get used to the Thai method. However, when they did, they found that happy working relationships could be maintained. Sometimes we need to go a long way from home to appreciate the delicate art of dealing with people.

ONE of my friends is the headmaster of a mixed school, and the other day he observed a boy repeatedly hitting a girl of about the same age with a long stick.

At last she managed to grab the stick and pull it out of his hands.

Was she about to give him a taste of his own medicine? No. She calmly broke the stick into small pieces across her knee and threw them away.

My friend told me about the incident because he thought that girl is going to have a great deal to contribute to society when she grows up — and I agree with him.

COUNTRY CALM

THE FRIENDSHIP BOOK

THERE have been many poems written about April. Here is an appealing one I had not seen before. It is by the London poet, Joyce Frances Carpenter:

> She laughs through raindrops as we pass
> And touches us with little things,
> Soft tender leaves, and tiny wings,
> Then hides with violets in the grass.
>
> She sings with blackbirds at daybreak
> And dances in the morning breeze.
> Pink apple blossom on the trees
> Is icing for her birthday cake.
>
> Young April starts off with a smile
> And laughs at us on All Fools' Day;
> "Be happy now," she seems to say,
> "I stay for just a little while".

WHEN he was young, my friend David's hobby was fretwork, and many an hour he spent fashioning wood into models and carvings. One plaque he made, hangs on my wall today, valuable not only as a reminder of him and our friendship, but also for the message it conveys:

> TODAY
> IS THE TOMORROW
> WE WORRIED ABOUT YESTERDAY
> AND ALL IS WELL.

Words of hope and comfort indeed.

THE FRIENDSHIP BOOK

HERE is some good advice from the poet Anne Kreer:

> *If you don't speak to strangers,*
> *You'll never make new friends,*
> *So break the ice,*
> *And say "hello",*
> *See what a glow it lends*
> *To skies that have been overcast,*
> *To heavens that were so grey;*
> *Just say "hello" to strangers,*
> *And make new friends today.*

THE earth is the Lord's, and all that therein is; the compass of the world, and they that dwell therein.   Psalms 24,1.

I HAVE a paperweight which has saved many a flurry when a door or window has been opened. However, mine is only an ordinary one, and quite different to that used by John Ruskin, the famous writer and critic. He had a beautiful stone paperweight on which was carved the single word *TODAY.* He took this as his own personal motto — the word on the paperweight was a constant reminder that each day was a great gift from God, to be used loyally, faithfully and usefully.

It's said that we learn from the past, which is true, but we cannot re-live yesterday. As for tomorrow . . . well, who knows? I believe if we take Ruskin's motto and live today as best we can, then that is the best preparation for tomorrow.

THE FRIENDSHIP BOOK

THOSE who have become acquainted with Sheila Hocken and her guide dog through her book "Emma and I" must have been both moved and inspired by her story.

Sheila inherited defective eyesight from her parents and went completely blind whilst in her teens. Emma, her Labrador, became her eyes and a remarkable and fulfilling relationship developed between them which enabled Sheila to lead a happy and active life.

Many years later, an operation restored Sheila's sight completely. Writing about this experience, she said, "The sunshine burst in on me and I imagined the birth of the world. Of course I knew that it had been like this for millions of years, but I still felt it was the entire Creation suddenly laid on for my personal benefit."

She has never lost that sense of wonder. When she hears people complaining about trivial things, she wants to remind them how lucky they are to be able to see the sky and the clouds and all the beautiful things around them.

We may not have shared Sheila Hocken's experience, but haven't we all got so many things for which to be grateful?

"HOW old are you?" a small boy was asked. "I'm not old," was the reply. "I'm six!"

If we have the right outlook we can give a similar reply at any age, can't we? I have a friend who, because of her vitality and optimism could answer that question quite truthfully, saying, "I'm not old — I'm 86!"

THURSDAY—APRIL 20.

FRANCES HAVERGAL, well known as the writer of many lovely hymns including "Who is on the Lord's side?" left behind in her memoirs these reasons for going to church:

1. God has blessed the Lord's day and hallowed it, making no exceptions for hot, cold or stormy days.

2. I expect my minister to be there. I should be surprised if he were to stay at home on account of the weather.

3. By staying away I may lose the prayers which may bring God's blessing and the sermon that would have done me great good.

4. On any important business, rainy weather does not keep me at home and Church attendance is in God's sight very important.

5. Such weather will show me on what foundation my faith is built, it will prove to me how much I love Christ. True love rarely fails to meet an appointment.

6. I know not how many Sundays more God may give me and it would be a poor preparation for my first Sunday in Heaven to have slighted my last Sunday on earth.

FRIDAY—APRIL 21.

I WAS looking through an old autograph album recently and was amused by this anonymous verse:

The night was rough, and cold and blough,
She hid her hands inside her mough.
It chilled her through, what could she dough?
And still the wind the stronger blough.
And yet although there was no snough,
The weather was a cruel blough.
It made her cough, please do not scough,
She coughed until her hat blew ough.

D

SPRING SPLENDOUR

E

A FRIEND was telling the Lady of the House that she had been to London, and had seen the Changing of the Guard. She recalls that it was pouring rain. Near her stood an Italian woman, her headscarf sopping wet and water streaming down her coat. Instinctively, Jennie apologised to her for our awful weather.

To her surprise, the visitor said, "I really like it this way. In Venice, where I live, it's often far too hot. It's lovely not to see the sun."

It reminded me that in the Canadian city of Vancouver they often call rain "liquid sunshine" — a delightful phrase.

There has to be a bright lining in every cloud, hasn't there?

VERILY, verily, I say unto you, If a man keep my saying, he shall never see death.   John 8,51.

OUR neighbour Marjorie has just spent a few days in hospital and was deeply impressed by the patience and cheerfulness of the nursing staff.

One evening she had said to a young nurse, "You look tired, my dear."

"Well, it *has* been a long day," the young woman admitted but without any suggestion of complaint.

"You have to be on your feet such a lot, don't you?" said Marjorie.

The nurse smiled. "Well, I suppose feet are meant to be 'on', aren't they?"

THE FRIENDSHIP BOOK

THE Lady of the House reminded me recently of this saying which we first came across many years ago: "Where there is no love, pour love in, and you will draw love out."

These words from John of the Cross, the Spanish mystic, are as true today as they were when they were written.

CYRIL ARTHUR PEARSON was born at Wookey in Somerset where his father was curate. As Cyril grew up, he loved to read and write and soon developed a flair for journalism.

He went to work in London — in Fleet Street — where his talent flourished, and Cyril Arthur Pearson eventually gave his readers the "Daily Express", "Pearson's Weekly" and "Pearson's Magazine".

At the height of his career in 1913, he became blind. He hardly knew what to do once the door was shut on his reading and writing, and he had many a dark hour of despair. However, he never gave up, but instead offered his disability to God — and God told him what to do. Cyril founded St Dunstan's, the home where blinded soldiers in the First World War were given every care and attention.

Today, at Ian Fraser House in Ovingdean, Sussex, facilities are still available through St Dunstan's to rehabilitate blind men and women from the Forces. They are trained for employment, and helped to adjust to their handicap and develop new interests.

Cyril Arthur Pearson would have been very proud of this achievement. The Lord brought light into his own darkness and it has spread to others, bringing a new dimension of hope to their lives.

PRECIOUS TIMES

One of Summer's bounties,
It cannot be denied,
Is a quiet family outing
By a peaceful waterside.

THE FRIENDSHIP BOOK

I WAS very taken with this verse by Brian A. Wren entitled "A Thought". It helps to make me aware of the many ordinary things around me that can give pleasure.

> *Life is great, so sing about it,*
> *As we can and as we should;*
> *Shops and buses, towns and people,*
> *Village, farmland, field and wood.*
> *Life is great and life is given,*
> *Life is lovely, free and good.*

As Montaigne wrote in his "Essays", "The value of life lies not in the length of days, but in the use we make of them; a man may live long, yet get little from life. Whether you find satisfaction in life depends not on your tale of years, but on your will."

B AKEWELL tarts are a favourite in many families, but I wonder how many of us are aware that what we enjoy was all due to somebody's mistake?

It was 1859 when the cook at the Rutland Arms in Bakewell was making a strawberry tart for the guests' lunch. In her hurry, she put in the strawberry jam first in place of the sponge mixture she'd intended. Rather than start all over again, she topped it with the sponge mixture.

She thought there might be complaints, but, instead, the guests complimented the landlady on the delicious new creation, and the cook was instructed to keep on making them in the same way.

The Pudding Shop in Bakewell still has the famous tarts for sale, a nice reminder that success *can* come from our mistakes!

SATURDAY—APRIL 29.

"GARDEN of Memories" is the title of this delightful poem by the Welsh poet, Glynfab John. What a lovely picture it conjures up! I'm sure you'll agree that there's nothing more pleasing to the eye than a flower-filled garden.

> My grandfather tended
>   His flower garden well,
> And each petal's perfume
>   I still seem to smell.
>
> Daffodils and tulips
>   Bloomed with snowdrops so small,
> While crocuses clustered
>   By the ivy-clad wall.
>
> Nasturtiums and pansies
>   Massed closely beside
> Lily of the valley
>   And staid London pride.
>
> Sweet honeysuckle
>   Rivalled night-scented stocks;
> Hydrangeas and lupins
>   Jostled tall hollyhocks.
>
> And near the backyard
>   Grew a trim lilac-tree,
> Whose blossoms in May
>   Shed their fragrance — for me.

SUNDAY—APRIL 30.

BLESSED be the Lord God of Israel; for he hath visited and redeemed his people.   Luke 1,68.

MAY

MONDAY—MAY 1.

WORRY seems a common malady nowadays, and many cures have been suggested for it, but one of the shortest and simplest I have come across was a verse under the heading, "A Thought for the Week" in a local church magazine:

That man is blest
Who does his best,
And leaves the rest
And doesn't worry!

TUESDAY—MAY 2.

MRS CLARK was scolding her husband for forgetting her birthday:

"Why can't a man think of his wife a few years after marriage as he did before? It's just too bad! You've forgotten my birthday *again*. Only a few years ago, you declared that the date was engraved on your heart and you never failed to give me a present. Why not today?"

"My dear, I didn't wish to remind you that you are a year older," came the disarming reply.

WEDNESDAY—MAY 3.

THROUGHOUT the centuries, the Chinese have been noted for the wisdom of their philosophers and much of it has been distilled in the form of proverbs.

Here is one, new to me, that could be of great encouragement when we have to face some task which seems almost insuperable: *The man who removed the mountain began by carrying away small stones.*

HOUSEPROUD

THE FRIENDSHIP BOOK

OLD GEORGE, as he was affectionately known, was a much respected Methodist local preacher in the Yorkshire Dales.

No-one had ever heard George grumble or complain, but there came an occasion when some people thought it was more than likely he would.

He was to preach in a remote chapel, on a Sunday when the snow lay deep and the wind was keen and biting. Old George trudged up the hill from the nearest bus stop and, shivering with cold, proceeded to get ready for the service.

"He won't find anything optimistic to say today," thought the congregation as he entered the pulpit. They had reckoned without George.

"Let us pray," he began, and then, "We thank thee, Lord, that every day is not like this one!"

YOU may have heard of the boy whose teacher asked him to tell her what he knew about electricity.

He replied, very briefly, "I don't know what it is, but I know what it does."

Happiness is rather like that, isn't it? We don't know just what causes it, but we do know the results.

Professor Robert Rainy was a famous minister last century. He used to tell how, one day at breakfast, his little granddaughter announced, "Grandfather goes to Heaven every night."

"How do you know?" her parents asked.

"Because he always wakes up looking so happy," she said simply.

I think she put in a nutshell what clever men have written books trying to explain.

THE FRIENDSHIP BOOK

MOHAMMED AJEEB was a teenager when he arrived in this country from his native Pakistan more than 30 years ago. He found himself on a London-bound train in freezing weather conditions, but in the company of a genial Englishman who warmed to the young immigrant and did his best to help. He managed to adjust the heating so that the temperature was at least bearable, put his own overcoat around the young stranger's shoulders, and bought him a cup of cocoa. In fact, he even offered to find the young man a job.

When they reached London, their ways parted. The youngster managed to land a job, worked hard and eventually became a successful businessman in Bradford. In May 1985 he was elected Lord Mayor, the town's first chief citizen from another country. It was no mean achievement from such humble beginnings.

Mr Ajeeb had never forgotten the man who had befriended him on his first day in England. He didn't know his name. Indeed, all he knew about him was that he was a farmer in Derbyshire. However, he eventually tracked him down. The Good Samaritan on the train turned out to be the late Ted Moult, the popular broadcaster, and he had forgotten all about his kindness and compassion to a young stranger so many years ago.

I am reminded of the old saying, "Never forget a kindness done *to* you, but forget any done *by* you."

HE Loveth righteousness and judgement: the earth is full of the goodness of the Lord.

Psalms 33,5.

THE FRIENDSHIP BOOK

MONDAY—MAY 8.

SOME Lancashire youngsters were listening to a rather pompous individual who was speaking to a Sunday School class on the subject of self-sacrifice.

"Can you tell me what has made me leave my snug fireside and come out into the cold to address you on a day like this?" he asked.

"Aye, I can," said one of the lads. "It's because tha likes to hear thyself talk!"

TUESDAY—MAY 9.

PRAYER is the burden of a sigh,
The falling of a tear,
The upward glancing of an eye
When none but God is near.

Isn't that a lovely verse? I'm told that it's the one that Queen Victoria kept by her bedside at Osborne House, on the Isle of Wight.

When she was widowed, Victoria often suffered great loneliness. At those times, only her deep faith sustained her — that and her strong sense of duty to the country and the people she served.

WEDNESDAY—MAY 10.

SIR ALEC GUINNESS, that splendid actor, told how his friend Sir Tyrone Guthrie had a phrase for everything that wasn't quite right. It could apply to toothache or the loss of all the company's costumes while on tour.

It was just three words: "Rise above it".

I think you will agree that if we all faced troubles and disappointments in that frame of mind, many of them would vanish.

Put it to the test some time. Just say, "Rise above it"!

LEGACY

Everyone loves a quiet spot to dream the hours away,
And a friend to share
The beauty there
In the peace of a Summer's day.

Wherever lies your Eden — and only you may know —
You'll want to raise
A hymn of praise
To Him who made it so.

THURSDAY—MAY 11.

READERS will recognise the scene set by this evocative poem — the end of cold, chilly days and the start of brighter, warmer weather heralding a fresh start to life. Read them this May morning and be glad!

> With shining light
>   Of daffodils,
> With soothing green
>   Of woods and hills,
> Wild grasses and
>   The cuckoo's song,
> May tells us that
>   The Winter's gone!
>
> Now everywhere
>   Through once bare earth,
> Small tender shoots
>   Have thrust to birth,
> And manifest in
>   Maytime flowers
> Fulfilment of
>   The trusting hours.

Joyce Frances Carpenter.

FRIDAY—MAY 12.

WE have often been told — and, I hope, discovered from our own experience — that the way to relieve our own burdens and anxieties is to lose ourselves in doing something for someone else.

However, I wonder whether it has ever been expressed as movingly as by the Danish philosopher, Soren Kierkegaard, who simply said, "The door to happiness opens outwards."

THE FRIENDSHIP BOOK

THE stress and pressure of everyday living can be very wearing. Here are three thoughtful verses by a writer who understands life's trials — and how to withstand them:

Rest will often come to us at evening, when we pray,
However simple are the words that we have knelt to say,
And if we take a well-loved book, and turn its pages through,
How often we can lose ourselves for just an hour or two.

Rest may come with someone dear, a friendly little chat,
A joke, a laugh, a new idea, talk of this and that,
Or, walking through the woods at dawn, to hear the blackbird sing,
Brings music to our tired hearts, and gentle comforting.

So rest, dear friend, when life becomes almost too much to bear,
Find comfort in the simple joys that meet us everywhere,
The robin with his bright red breast, the lark in skies of blue,
In all these small, but lovely things, rest comes to me and you.

Margaret H. Dixon.

DELIGHT then in the Lord: and he shall give thee thy heart's desire. Psalms 37,4.

MONDAY—MAY 15.

RECENTLY the Lady of the House and I were travelling in a train and as we passed a village school a group of children were sitting on the wall waving to the passengers.

As the Lady of the House waved back to them smilingly, she said, "You know, Francis, I always wave back because I remember a group of us, when we were children, waving like that, and nobody took any notice."

Such a simple thing, but what a difference it makes when a wave, a smile, a cheerful greeting is exchanged. Try it, and see!

TUESDAY—MAY 16.

I CAME across this quotation by Mark Twain recently and I thought how apt it was:

When some men discharge an obligation, you can hear the discharge for miles around.

WEDNESDAY—MAY 17.

AT the end of his sermon recently, our minister concluded, "Yes, when we cut the thread that holds us in living touch with the Unseen above, we fall."

His comment reminded me of an old Dutch fable which tells how a spider slid down a single thread of web from the high roof timbers of a barn, and settled himself on a lower level. There he spread his web, caught flies, lived well, and grew fat. Then, one day, walking about his domain, he saw the thread that stretched up into the heights above him, and thought how useless it seemed, so he snapped it. His web collapsed and the spider was trodden underfoot.

E

THE FRIENDSHIP BOOK

DYSLEXIA is a word most of us had never heard of 20 years ago. As you read this page, your eyes flash a message to your brain with the words in the correct order, but if you suffer from dyslexia, your eyes will send the brain a jumbled message and reading will be very difficult.

Beryl Reid, the actress, once told how she coped with dyslexia. When she is taking part in a play, the other actors have their scripts to refer to. She has to memorise her part.

We know how well she has overcome her handicap and admire her for it. I think we should admire, too, her answer when she was asked what kind of work she liked best.

"Whatever I'm doing at the moment," was her prompt reply.

Wouldn't you agree that the happiest people are those who can give just that answer?

JOHN WESLEY, that magnificent preacher, was also a modest man and he made it known that he did not wish anyone to write his life story either while he was alive, or even after his death. All the same, the founder of the Methodist Church could not prevent a biography of himself being written — the world had to be told of his great ministry and influence.

In fact, none of us can prevent our biography being written — it may not be in print, but it will certainly be recorded. It is constantly being written in the lives of other people — every word, every action, deeds of kindness or unkindness — they all make their mark in the hearts and minds of folk around us, marks remembered long after we're gone.

F

THE FRIENDSHIP BOOK

ALL mothers, particularly those with grown-up children, will recognise the sentiments expressed in this charming poem:

It only seems like yesterday I heard your first weak cry,
You gave me many busy days — no time to sit and sigh,
And then the thrill to see you stand and slowly walk to me,
The enchanting sound of baby talk as I nursed you on my knee.

It only seems like yesterday that you went off to school,
I sat all day and worried so — but you appeared so cool;
Remembering all the sports days, the pride when you had won
They really were such happy days of laughter, love and fun.

This morning you are starting work, the years pass like a dream,
My little boy no longer — a youth of seventeen,
Another chapter in your life is just about to start,
I wish for you contentment and peace within your heart,
I pray the Lord will guide you and keep you safe each day,
And thank Him now with gratitude as you go on life's way.

Maralyn I. Fawcett-Smith.

THEREFORE with joy shall ye draw water out of the wells of salvation.   Isaiah 12,3.

THE FRIENDSHIP BOOK

MONDAY—MAY 22.

A NORTHAMPTONSHIRE Women's Institute ran a competition a little while ago to find "the most useless gadget in your kitchen". It was won by the member who submitted a photograph of her husband!

TUESDAY—MAY 23.

I CONFESS that I had never heard of Celia Laighton Thaxter until I came across her name at the foot of a verse on a calendar of daily quotations, but though I may forget her name I don't think I shall easily forget her verse:

> *Sad soul, take comfort, nor forget,*
> *That sunrise never failed us yet.*

WEDNESDAY—MAY 24.

BEFORE he became one of the best-loved Presidents of the United States of America, James Garfield was the Principal of Hiram College in Ohio, a college designed to give youngsters from the farms of the Western Reserve the chance of an academic education.

One father brought along his son, and wanted to see the syllabus — the usual preparatory course lasted four years. After inspecting it, he said, "Mr Garfield, I don't believe my son will have time to take all that. Could you provide him with a shorter course?"

"Yes, I think I can," replied Garfield. "You see, it all depends on what you want to make of him. When God wants to make an oak, He takes hundreds of years; but when He wants to make a vegetable plant, it requires only three months."

THE FRIENDSHIP BOOK

IZAAK WALTON, the 17th century Derbyshire man, spent many hours fishing by the River Dove in happy contemplation. The beauty and tranquillity of his surroundings must have coloured his attitude to life and is reflected in his book "The Compleat Angler".

Among his wise words I came across this: "Be sure your face is towards the light. Let the sun shine on your face and your shadow fall behind you. Blessed is the angler of the sunlit face and of the shadow unseen."

What Walton was pointing out was that if the angler's shadow fell across the water, the fish would be frightened away. But it's a message for living, too. If we let all the little irritations, resentments and upsets fall behind us, we can face the world with a sunny outlook, making life pleasanter for everybody.

MANY people were sorry when the familiar sixpence ceased to be legal tender. It is perhaps difficult to realise nowadays that this humble coin was the means of paying for the building of one of London's most beautiful landmarks — St Paul's Cathedral.

At the time when plans were agreed for the building of the cathedral, every ton of coal brought into the Port of London was subject to a sixpenny tax. All the money obtained in this way went towards the building of St Paul's.

The old sixpence is equal to a mere two and a half pence today, but isn't it wonderful to think that this great cathedral owes its origin to the collection of one tiny sixpence after another?

THE WAY AHEAD

THE FRIENDSHIP BOOK

A RATHER shabby-looking man came forward to serve a customer in a Dutch shop. Nothing odd about that really, but the customer would have been amazed at that assistant's topsy-turvy life!

Not long before, he had been the master, and his present boss had been his servant. He had also been famous as an artist.

Rembrandt Harmensz van Rijn was born in Leyden in 1606, the son of a miller. In 1631, after training as an artist, he moved to Amsterdam and became well-known all over Europe. His pictures brought him large sums of money, but as fast as money came in, it went out again, on other paintings, on generous gifts to friends and acquaintances.

A slump in the art world resulted in his bankruptcy. The only possessions he had left were a Bible and two foot-warmers. Yet he did not despair. His son Titus stood by him and so did his former servant, Stoffels, who employed him as a shop assistant.

It was only after the death of Stoffels in 1664 and Titus in 1668 that the artist really felt despair. He died on 18th October 1669 in poverty and regarded by many as a failure. Yet his Dutch interior paintings and his religious pictures such as "Descent from the Cross" and "Christ Heals the Sick" are now priceless.

In life, poverty; after death, an immense art legacy.

T HE Lord bless thee, and keep thee: The Lord make his face shine upon thee, and be gracious unto thee: The Lord lift up his countenance upon thee, and give thee peace. — Numbers 6,24-26.

THE FRIENDSHIP BOOK

I SMILED when the Lady of the House told me of a conversation she'd overheard.

Two little girls had been playing at doctors and nurses, and one said to the other, "When I grow up I'm going to marry a doctor and then I can be ill for nothing."

The other little girl, not wishing to be outdone, retorted, "When I grow up I'm going to marry a minister and then I can be good for nothing!"

THERE'S a time for holding on,
And a time for letting go,
A time for acquiescing,
And a time for saying "no".

And always the decision
Is entirely up to you;
Just ask your conscience —
It will tell you
What you ought to do.

Anne Kreer.

MY grandmother lived in the days when families tended to be larger than today. In her thirties she was left a widow with seven children to bring up. It couldn't have been easy but through it all she kept cheerful and she kept her family cheerful, too. If sometimes even necessities seemed in short supply she was fond of saying, "We're short of nothing we have got!"

No wonder she survived all her troubles. A philosophy like that is surely unconquerable.

JUNE

THURSDAY—JUNE 1.

ONE lovely Summer's day in the early years of this century, a party of tourists was sailing down the Potomac River. One man had a fine voice and had just sung the old familiar hymn "Jesu, lover of my soul".

A fellow-passenger asked if he had ever fought in the Civil War. The singer said he had — under the command of General Grant.

His companion replied, "Well, I was very close to you one bright night when you were on guard duty. I crept near your post to finish you off and as you paced back and forth, you were humming that tune. I raised my gun to shoot, but then I heard some of the words you were singing — 'Cover my defenceless head with the shadow of Thy wing'. Your prayer was answered. I could not shoot you after that."

FRIDAY—JUNE 2.

HE criticised her puddings and he didn't like her cake.
He wished she'd make the biscuits that his mother used to bake.
She didn't wash the dishes and she didn't make the stew,
She didn't mend his socks as his mother used to do:
Oh, well, she was not perfect, though she tried to do her best,
Until at last she thought it was time she had a rest.
So one day when he said the same old rigmarole all through,
She turned and boxed his ears — just as his mother used to do!

SATURDAY—JUNE 3.

I MET a member of the SS the other day. He is one of the most cheerful souls I know, always trying to encourage others. His wife gladly pays tribute to the confidence, hope and humour he instils into her. His homespun wisdom never ceases to amaze her.

He calls himself just an ordinary chap, nothing special, but I happen to know that he is seldom free from pain—even though you never hear him complain.

As I said, he is a member of the SS—the Silent Sufferers.

SUNDAY—JUNE 4.

FOR God hath not given us the spirit of fear; but of power, and of love, and of a sound mind.

Timothy II 1,7.

MONDAY—JUNE 5.

RUTH is one of those country lasses who are the salt of the earth, and she has been a good friend of the Lady of the House for many years.

One day I came across her baking bread, something she has always enjoyed doing. She also loves to share her baking with other people. Her husband jokes that it cannot possibly be cheaper for her to bake her own bread, because she is always giving it away!

"Well," smiles Ruth, "that is what my mother used to do, and I can't help being like her. I get so much pleasure from giving to others."

It made me think of the words of our Lord — "God loves a cheerful giver." Ruth is cheerful, and most certainly a giver.

TUESDAY—JUNE 6.

ON his way to work each day, businessman Allan Thompson had to walk past the trim cottage of old Andrew, a dedicated gardener. One sunny June morning, Allan, en route for his usual bus, was surprised to see Andrew hard at work cutting his hedge.

"You're starting early today, Andrew!" Allan remarked.

"Starting?" The old man paused for a moment. "I'm nearly finished! Couldn't waste a fine morning like this, so I rose at five."

At 75, Andrew still possessed a great zest for life. He was getting the most out of life by putting his best into it.

WEDNESDAY—JUNE 7.

I LIKE the story of the young preacher who was invited to a small country church. He had spent a lot of time preparing a sermon, and was somewhat disappointed to find that his congregation consisted of one elderly farmer.

The young man asked him if he still wanted to hear the sermon.

The farmer thought for a moment and then he answered slowly, "Well, if I took a bucketful of meal down to the yard and only one hen showed up, I'd still feed her."

So the preacher launched into his sermon, which lasted the best part of an hour. When he finished, he asked the farmer what he thought of it. Again the farmer deliberated, and then he said, "Well, if I took a bucketful of meal down to the yard and only one hen showed up, I'd feed her — but I'm blowed if I'd give her the whole bucketful!"

THE FRIENDSHIP BOOK

ON 17th March 1908, a new type of children's publication appeared in bookshops. It was the first part of "The Children's Encyclopaedia", which many older readers will remember with affection.

It was the brain-child of a man who had no University education, but left school at an early age to become a printer's copy-holder. Arthur Mee was born at Stapleford, near Nottingham. After the family's removal to Nottingham itself, he was trained as a journalist on a city newspaper.

Although his early education had been basic, he was for ever educating himself by reading, asking questions and taking a keen interest in all types of subjects. What is more, he possessed the knack of passing on the information to others, particularly children.

He founded "The Children's Newspaper" which had, as its slogan, "To make goodness news". His own motto was, "The more we love beauty the more beautiful we are".

When he died in 1943, his last request was that nobody should send flowers to his funeral, but give what they could afford to a hospital that cared for sick or handicapped children. The gift was to be marked "For Arthur Mee".

THE headmaster walked to school with eight-year-old Mark, and in the course of conversation asked him where he was going for his holidays.

"Cockermouth, sir," came the reply.

"Ah, and who was born at Cockermouth?" asked the Head, thinking of the poet William Wordsworth.

"My mum," was the proud reply.

SATURDAY—JUNE 10.

THE world-famous French cellist, Paul Tortelier, holds strong views not only about music, but much else, too, especially world peace. However, he believes that people ought not to try to force their views on others.

He says he has never forgotten some words he heard long ago: "When you look at a cup someone hands to you, the handle is on your right, but to them it is on the left!"

How true it is that there are two sides to every question.

SUNDAY—JUNE 11.

AND the whole earth was of one language, and of one speech.   Genesis 11,1.

MONDAY—JUNE 12.

IT was a very hot Saturday and the Trooping of the Colour was taking place in London. The Mall was lined with guardsmen standing stiffly to attention, but suddenly, one of them was observed to be swaying in the overpowering heat.

Not quite knowing what to do, the officer in charge had a word with a nearby policeman, who wasn't under such formal discipline. The man in blue walked up to the sweltering guardsman, felt in his pocket for what he felt sure would be there — and found it.

He unwrapped the barley sugar, popped it into the guardsman's mouth, and returned to his post. And as a result, the ranks of guardsmen standing to attention remained erect and unbroken. A simple act had saved the day.

SURPRISE

Sometimes, when we least expect it,
Round an unfamiliar bend,
There's a little glimpse of heaven —
And, perhaps, a new-found friend.

THE FRIENDSHIP BOOK

DR Samuel Johnson, the famous 18th century writer, had opinions on most things — epitaphs included. He said, "Those epitaphs are therefore the most perfect which set virtue in the strongest light and are best adapted to exalt the reader's ideals and raise his emulation."

He would certainly have given top marks to the 19th century Yorkshire epitaph in Pudsey churchyard to a young wife:

Behold the silent tomb it doth embrace
A virtuous wife with Rachel's lovely face,
Sarah's obedience, Lydia's open heart,
Martha's care, but Mary's better part.

Appreciation would surely also have gone to the epitaph to Mary Brown who died in 1823 and is buried in Flamborough churchyard, Yorkshire:

She was — but words are wanting to say what,
Think what a wife should be — and she was that!

SOMETIMES when the Lady of the House and I visit stately homes with their great expanses of smooth, green lawns I come home rather enviously to my own small patch of grass.

However, I read something recently which made me look at my little lawn with a new sense of wonder. The writer said that nine out of every ten plants on earth are grass of some kind and that it has been around for thousands of years. A simple enough thought, reminding me that my grass is ordinary, yet at the same time wonderful. And it strikes me that this is a good way of looking at many of the common things of life — there is *something* wonderful about them all.

THE FRIENDSHIP BOOK

IT has been said that a true gentleman always tries to avoid giving embarrassment to others. If this description is true, composer Sir Edward Elgar surely merits the title.

Once he was a guest of honour at a performance of his "Dream of Gerontius" and was seated next to the Lord Mayor of Manchester, who had arrived so late there had been no time for introductions. After the performance had been in progress for a while, the Lord Mayor whispered to him, "Dull music this, isn't it?"

Not wanting to embarrass him, the composer nodded in agreement, and then at the interval before the Mayor would have time to realise who he was sitting beside, Elgar rose, saying he had to leave.

"That's all right, old chap," came the reply. "I only wish to goodness I could come with you!"

AT the end of the American Civil War, General Robert E. Lee was walking past a house in the front garden of which were the disfigured remains of a tree half-ruined by enemy artillery fire.

"What am I to do about it?" demanded the owner of the house.

"Cut it down, my dear madam, and forget it," was the General's reply.

It was in keeping with his philosophy at that time, for he was working hard to heal the nation's bitter wounds by urging them to forget the past and concentrate on building a brighter future.

Resentment of the past *can* blur our vision for the future. Best to cut out the useless deadwood in our minds, and replace it with forward-looking thoughts.

THE FRIENDSHIP BOOK

I OFTEN have cause to remember one of the stories broadcast in a popular BBC radio series, "Five to Ten". It concerned a Mr McKay of Edinburgh who noticed a small, unfortunate boy with his legs in irons near Waverley Station.

An hour later, Mr McKay was climbing a flight of steep steps that led towards the Castle when he was surprised to see the disabled lad ahead of him. The boy was out of breath and obviously finding the climb difficult, but when Mr McKay offered to help him he shook his head and grinned.

"Do you know," he said, "I've never climbed as high as this before. It's the biggest adventure of my life!"

So Mr McKay's good deed for the day was to pass the boy, leaving him to struggle on with his "biggest adventure".

I CAN do all things through Christ which strengtheneth me.   Philippians 4,13.

C. E. MONTAGUE has a short story about a small boy who had the priceless privilege of a very happy home. Each night as he nestled down into bed he would sigh contentedly and murmur sleepily, "Fun tomorrow!"

I forget the rest of the story and, of course, life can't all be fun, but surely there is enough of goodness and gladness about to enable us to end each day as that small boy did, with eager hopes for tomorrow.

F

THE FRIENDSHIP BOOK

I HAVE been writing a reference for a young man who hopes to start an apprenticeship in the Forces. I wrote that I've known him and his family for 12 years and that nobody could ask for better neighbours. I said that Peter is honest, hard-working and cheerful. I would like to have said more, to have told how I have seen him develop from a happy-go-lucky boy to a considerate young man. I would love to have included things like the way Peter sweeps the snow off our path without our knowledge, the time he came to say he hoped he hadn't kept us awake after the party he'd had when his parents were away, how he offered to help in the garden though we know he hates gardening.

As I say, you can't put these things into a reference to be read by people in an office far away. It's a pity, isn't it? However, I've done my best for him, though, really, I don't think Peter needs a reference from me or anyone else. He is his own best reference, and is sure to get on well in the world.

I HAVE quoted before from "A Thought For The Week" on a church service paper which a friend sends me from time to time. Not long ago they had a short series of sayings by great Christians.

One that impressed me very much was from the fourth century African bishop of Hippo, Augustine:

> To my God, a heart of flame;
> To my fellow-men, a heart of love;
> To myself, a heart of steel.

No wonder Augustine is numbered among the saints!

G

THE FRIENDSHIP BOOK

AFTER encouraging millions of people to give millions of pounds to feed the starving nations of Africa, Bob Geldof met Mother Teresa.

You could scarcely imagine a bigger contrast — the pop star working in the glare of publicity to reach his object and the frail little woman working night and day to bring comfort to the dying in the slums of Calcutta.

Each of them, however, recognised the greatness in the other. Bob Geldof described her as a "tiny giant" and likes to repeat her words to him: "I can do things you cannot do. You can do things I cannot do. But we must both do it."

Encouragement, surely, for all of us who think the little we can do is really not worth doing.

IN bygone days many a man was remembered long after he'd died because he had built a bridge across a dangerous river.

One such person was James Black, who built a bridge over 280 years ago. If you stand on the Gannochy Bridge, near Edzell, in Angus, you will be thrilled by the scenery in the rocky ravine.

Before James Black built his bridge, the only way of crossing was by a dangerous ford. He decided where a bridge could be built, and at his own expense and with the help of only one other man, he built one. Though it has since been widened, it was in the beginning, one man's dream and has continued to serve a vital purpose for travellers.

James Black's tombstone bears these words:
No bridge on earth can be a bridge to heaven,
Yet let to generous deed due praise be given.

THE FRIENDSHIP BOOK

SATURDAY—JUNE 24.

THE Lady of the House came in one day, her eyes shining with enthusiasm. She had been to a meeting of our local fellowship.

"Was it a good talk?" I asked.

"Oh, yes. It was by Mrs Watson. I didn't know her father had been a lighthouse keeper. She was telling us how the family went with him round Scotland from one lighthouse to another. They moved so often that she attended six different schools.

"But you know what impressed me most? It was a rule that a Bible should be provided in every lighthouse, and when the lighthouse was a rock station, far from land, the head keeper was instructed to hold a short service every Sunday. Wasn't that a good idea?"

I pictured a Winter gale hurling itself against the stone tower and inside a voice, above the crash of the waves, reading words of comfort and inspiration. To me, that picture symbolises everything that is best in a service we all admire.

SUNDAY—JUNE 25.

THE Lord is my strength; and he is the wholesome defence of his Anointed. Psalms 28,9.

MONDAY—JUNE 26.

THE famous comedian, Arthur Askey, once fell off the stage on Clacton Pier. His fall was broken by the piano, but he hurt his back.

This is how he retold the story later: "They sent for an ambulance — but it took its time coming, so I nips up and does my turn while I'm waiting. I can't help it, I just have to go on . . ."

I know it wasn't a very wise thing to do, but that's the stuff real heroes are made of, isn't it?

TWO IN HARMONY

THE FRIENDSHIP BOOK

FAY INCHFAWN'S delightful books of poetry are perhaps not read as much nowadays as they were 50 years ago, which is a pity. A review of her work in "The Times" newspaper said, "We find something worth knowing in a woman who can think of God amid her groceries and praise Him in her scullery".

Here is a lovely verse from her poem "The Worshippers":

Draw nigh to God.
I needs must take
My apron off . . . and, first, I'll bake
These little pastries; then I'll spread
The tablecloth. I'll make my bed.
I'll tidy up and wash the floor,
And shake the mats, and lock the door.
When all is done, then I'll upstairs,
And reverently I'll say my prayers.

Draw nigh —
Lord, here am I.

WE are often urged to think and to act positively, and while this is obviously important in many situations, the famous writer E. M. Forster had a rather different idea. He wanted people to think negatively.

A surprising thing to say? Well, let's look at what he wrote:

"What the world most needs today are negative virtues — *not* minding people, *not* being huffy, touchy, irritable or revengeful."

You see his point?

THE FRIENDSHIP BOOK

MONUMENTS are usually erected only to the famous, but it is not so in the Staffordshire village of Rolleston, where there is a memorial to quite an ordinary man. The inscription reads:

"The Last Village Blacksmith 1904-1984".

When the horse was still the main source of transport, and particularly in a farming community, the blacksmith's shop was a most important part of village life. Horses had to be shod every three to four weeks and there was all the work of repairing broken farm implements and the maintenance of backyard pumps and so on.

Until recent years in Rolleston, you could still smell the acrid smoke from the forge and hear the heavy hammer on the anvil, but now all is quiet. The anvil has been removed to a small well-tended garden beside the bus shelter, and as folk pass by it, the inscription is a fitting reminder that it is not only the great who should be remembered with gratitude.

A YEAR or two ago, in the Highlands of Scotland, the Lady of the House and I watched a herd of red deer on a rocky mountainside. We were filled with admiration as they picked their way delicately over the rough ground.

I recalled a verse in one of the psalms: — *He maketh my feet like hind's feet, and setteth me upon my high places.* Lovely poetic words, but just what did the Psalmist mean? I think I understood as I watched those deer. Just as the hind is able to reach the heights in perfect safety, so we, if we do all things with all our strength, all our heart and all our soul, will also be able to achieve our greatest potential.

JULY

SATURDAY—JULY 1.

I LIKE the story of a small boy who had been looking forward to his Sunday School picnic for a long time. When the great day arrived, it was dull and wet. The outing was not a success. However, when he got back home and was ready for bed, he was determined to find something to be thankful for. In his prayers he said: "O God, thank you for giving me a chance to wear my new mackintosh."

SUNDAY—JULY 2.

GRACE be with all them that love our Lord Jesus Christ in sincerity. Amen.   Ephesians 6,24.

MONDAY—JULY 3.

LIFE wasn't always smooth for old Mrs Gilbert, but she kept smiling, and never let things get her down. When she died and her nephew was clearing out her house, he found the secret of her courage. By her bedside was a well-worn piece of paper bearing these lines:

> When ills and cares oppress you,
>   And you are dogged by fate,
> The heights seem far beyond your strength,
>   The hour now too late.
>
> 'Tis then a voice upholds you,
>   "Courage, be of hope,
> For I am with you and will guide
>   Your footsteps on the slope."

THE FRIENDSHIP BOOK

IT warms my heart when I learn of new attempts to bring our different church denominations closer together: local experiments in combined worship which often become regular, accepted events, neighbourly discussion meetings emphasising similarities rather than differences, and especially small, unsung acts of ordinary, loving individuals who live their lives apparently indifferent to the boundaries of their various fellowships.

One shining example of this latter group of people, who proves that a sense of humour also helps, is William Smith, who is locally dubbed, "Mr Ecumenical". Although he's a practising Anglican, he teaches in a Roman Catholic school and in his spare time he plays the trumpet in a Salvation Army band!

"Are there any complications to such a lifestyle?" I asked him.

"Only one," William replied with a twinkle in his eye. "My wife's a Strict Baptist. When I get home late at night, she ducks me in the bath!"

A STORY is told of an elderly preacher who was exhorting his congregation to give generously to the Lord's work. He was interrupted by a deacon who rose and said, "Parson, you have always told us that salvation is free — as free as the air we breathe and as free as the water in the river. If that is true, why are you always asking for money?"

The preacher adjusted his spectacles and solemnly replied, "Brother Jones, you are right. Salvation is free, but if you want water in your kitchen, you've got to have pipes and somebody has got to pay for the plumbing."

THE FRIENDSHIP BOOK

THE famous conductor, André Previn, believes in getting to know every member of his orchestra by name. He deplores the practice of some conductors who use at rehearsals impersonal terms such as "Flute" or "Trumpet".

"Players are people," he says, "not instruments."

What a splendid rule for ordinary life, too! Of course, there are people whose names we may not be able to get to know — the bus driver, the different people who serve us each time we go into a large store and so on. At least we can treat them as individuals and not as one of a faceless crowd. The personal touch in life really does make for a brighter day, both for us and those we're dealing with.

I WAS reading recently that our ancestors did without sugar until the 13th century; without coal fires until the 14th; without buttered bread until the 16th; without coffee, tea and soap until the 17th; without gas, matches and electricity until the 19th; without radio and television until the 20th.

It's food for thought, isn't it, in an acquisitive society that appears to value possessions more than it does people.

To quote a paraphrase of the words of Jesus, published by the World Council of Churches:

"I was hungry and starving and you were obese; thirsty and you were watering your garden; with no road to follow, and without hope, and you called the police and were happy that they took me a prisoner; barefoot and with ragged clothing and you were saying: 'I have nothing to wear, tomorrow I will buy something new'; sick and you asked: 'Is it infectious?'"

H

THE FRIENDSHIP BOOK

EVERY year I look forward to the display of delphiniums with their gorgeous spikes of blue, white or purple flowers, so I was very interested to hear, on a television gardening programme, that a Dutch horticulturist has been working for 30 years to perfect a red variety. At last his patience has succeeded, but it is said that it will take another ten years before they can be produced commercially.

It's a reminder of how much we owe, often without realising it, to the long and patient labour of others.

SURELY goodness and mercy shall follow me all the days of my life: and I will dwell in the house of the Lord for ever.   Psalms 23,6.
                                                    (Authorised Version)

MAUREEN BAKER from Great Ayton in Yorkshire puts into a few words the value of a good friend:

> It's comforting when trouble comes
> To share it with a friend,
> To talk it over bit by bit
> With someone who will spend —
> A while with you, until you see
> More clearly what to do,
> And strength and courage for the task
> Are somehow given you.
> Yes, trouble seems less hard to bear
> If someone will your burden share.

THE FRIENDSHIP BOOK

RECENTLY I received a letter from a friend in which she stated she believed in keeping busy in order to be happy.

Her comment is probably true for it is allied to the old saying that the busiest person always finds time for an extra job.

Mrs Roger Laycock in "Laycock of Lonedale", one of William Riley's novels, says, "Happiness is a plant that will grow in any soil that's watered by love and service, but withers in the hot sun of selfishness."

W. M. Thackeray wrote, "The world is a looking-glass and gives back to every man the reflection of his own face. Frown at it, and it in turn will look sourly at you; laugh at it and with it, and it is a jolly companion."

But the American author and essayist of the last century Ralph Waldo Emerson went even further by stating: "For every minute you are angry you lose 60 seconds of happiness."

I don't know the author of the following verse, but it contains a simple truth which can bring great happiness to ourselves and to others:

Don't be afraid to smile
On life's uncertain way,
It may be the only sunbeam
In someone's dreary day.

Don't be afraid to smile
On life's uneven track.
One little smile from you
And many are smiling back.

THE FRIENDSHIP BOOK

I LOVE to walk round some of the great gardens which generations of horticulturists have left as their everlasting memorial. Some time ago, the Lady of the House and I visited Castle Kennedy Gardens in Galloway, beautifully situated between two lochs, and with splendid vistas, daisy-sprinkled walks, drifts of rhododendrons and the Summer air heady with the scent of azaleas.

It set me thinking about gifts. Not many of us can leave a garden or a symphony for posterity, but haven't we all something to offer to make our world a better place, for ourselves and for others — however insignificant we may consider it to be?

As Abraham Lincoln said, "Die when I may, I want it said of me that I plucked a weed and planted a flower wherever I thought a flower would grow."

KEITH had just qualified as an architect, and he was impressing his grandfather with his knowledge. Norman and Tudor, Georgian and Baroque — he described all the styles with confidence.

"Have you a favourite architect, Grandad?" Keith asked.

The old man crossed to the window. "See that view in the distance?" he said. "Whoever designed that is my favourite architect."

"But there's nothing there but a few hills!" replied Keith.

"Aye, but somebody designed them and built them, just the same," came the reply. "And I'll tell you this — what's out there will still be standing when all your fine buildings have fallen to bits."

The oldest Architect of them all is still the best.

WILLING HANDS

Lessons learned through childhood play
In later life will smooth the way,
Assuring, with a ready smile,
We'll always go that extra mile.

THE FRIENDSHIP BOOK

ONE of Dr Donald Soper's greatest treasures is a carving of a little cross on a tiny pedestal.

It was given to him many years ago and he was told that the raw materials were a bit of ham bone left over from a meal, and a chunk of bakelite the craftsman had picked up — and it was all done with a cobbler's knife.

Despite the poor materials, it is a beautiful object and Dr Soper treasures it, all the more because it was carved, not by a famous craftsman, but an unknown prisoner in Pentonville Jail.

JESUS said unto him, If thou canst believe, all things *are* possible to him that believeth.

Mark 9,23.

MANY youngsters in the Methodist Church collect "missionary money" every week, and at the end of a year, those who have raised £10 or more are each presented with a certificate and a medal.

The presentation was being made one Sunday morning at a certain chapel when a little girl in the congregation whispered, "Mummy, I want to go and get one."

"No, darling!" came the reply. "They are only being given to the boys and girls who have been collecting during the last year."

"But I HAVE been collecting!" exclaimed Susan.

"Oh," said her mother, "and what have you collected, then?"

"Strawberries!" replied Susan.

THE FRIENDSHIP BOOK

THIS evocative poem by David Thomas captures the beauty to be found in a flower-filled Summer garden:

> There is no brighter, better place
>   My eye may ponder o'er,
> Than one small comely garden space
>   Before my cottage door.
>
> I talk with many a flower there
>   And smile upon them all,
> I breathe a fragrance in the air
>   Of Summer festival.
>
> Sweet violet and lavender
>   Respond to friendship true,
> Along with rose trees as they bear
>   Fine blooms of crimson hue.
>
> The tossing columbines display
>   A warmth of simple fun,
> And pansies deck the pebbled way
>   I love to walk upon.
>
> Such is the bright and happy place
>   My eye doth ponder o'er —
> The small and comely garden space
>   Before my cottage door.

A NEW vicar had arrived in the parish and one of the ladies in the congregation was asked how she liked him.

"Well, he's very nice," she replied, "but he doesn't hold me like the other one did."

THE FRIENDSHIP BOOK

THE bleak and windswept Holy Island of Lindisfarne, just off the coast of Northumberland, was where the revered and beloved Celtic saint, Cuthbert, chose to make his home. Here he lived alone, and, sick and weak though he often was, he forbade his followers on the mainland to visit him. One of his first acts on arrival was to build round his shelter a high circular wall of turf, so that he could see nothing of the mainland, or indeed the sea. All that was visible to him was the sky above, which to his pious mind represented Heaven itself.

Some 300 miles to the south-west of Lindisfarne is the bleak and windswept Cotswold village of Bisley, known locally as Bisley-God-Help-Us. It is very fortunate in having a magnificent old church, which can be reached by any one of four paths, the steepest of which has 51 steps. Inscribed deeply in the 33rd are the words: "SEEK THOSE THINGS WHICH ARE ABOVE". St. Cuthbert, looking down from his place in Heaven, must surely approve.

ON one occasion, Sir Harry Lauder was at Ibrox Park, entertaining a vast crowd before the arrival of Royalty, and when he had finished, he sat down on the dais next to the then General of the Salvation Army, Albert Orsborn.

"Ah, Salvation Army!" he exclaimed. "I've seen you all over the world — even in the South Sea Islands. I like you because you made the world sing!"

"But, Sir Harry," protested the General, "*you* have done that!"

"No," he declared emphatically, "I have only made it laugh; *you* have made it sing."

THE FRIENDSHIP BOOK

IT is not always easy to accept, but it is none the less true that it is often the hard experiences of life which strengthen our character.

While this is a familiar idea, I have rarely seen it as movingly expressed as in an anonymous verse which I came across recently:

It is the tautened string that music makes,
  It needs the doubt to prove the things that are;
The steel its temper from the furnace takes,
  Not sunshine, but the darkness shows the star.

SET Your affection on things above, not on things on earth.
                                    Colossians 3,2.

ISN'T it funny how we describe neighbours' actions compared with our own?

When *they* say what they think, they are called "spiteful". When *we* do the same, we are being "frank". When *they* don't like someone, they are "prejudiced". When *we* dislike someone, we are "good judges of human nature".

If *they* take time to do something, they are "dead slow". If *we* do likewise, we are "careful and deliberate". When *they* are nice to someone they are "toadying". When *we* do the same we are being "diplomatic".

It's worthwhile remembering that, from the other side of the fence, *you* are the neighbour!

THE FRIENDSHIP BOOK

HAVE you ever heard the legend of the two angels who fly between Heaven and earth?

The Angel of Prayer makes many journeys heavily laden with our requests. We ask for such a lot — health, peace, success and many other things.

The Angel of Gratitude, however, often returns from earth empty-handed.

Giving thanks never comes amiss, whether in hospital for attention and care given, to a colleague at work for moral support in a tricky situation, or to members of our own family for their love, help and concern.

No-one likes being taken for granted. A word of thanks or appreciation gives considerably more encouragement than the giver often realises.

FINDING a name for a new baby can be a problem, particularly when there are two sets of grandparents, each of whom has a name they would like the baby to bear.

The parents of Harry S. Truman, the US President during and after the war, had that problem. As a middle name for their son they had to choose between Solomon on one side and Shippe on the other. Whichever they chose to include in young Harry's name would hurt one set of grandparents or the other.

So they decided to call him Harry S. Truman. And what did the "S" stand for? Why, nothing but "S"!

I have never heard what the grandparents thought, but I've always considered Harry's parents were rather diplomatic!

THE FRIENDSHIP BOOK

NINEWELLS Hospital in Dundee is a wonderful place of healing, but it can also be a lonely place for a little boy who has just had his tonsils out and whose mother has had to leave him.

That's how it was for Alan until, noticing that he was ready to burst into tears, a young nurse hurried over and sat by his bedside. She picked up his book of fairytales, put her arm round him and began to read.

Little by little, the youngster fell under the spell of the words and in no time at all, he was nodding off. The grown-ups who were in the other beds in the small bay in the ward had been watching and listening with great attention. Two of them had put down the papers they were reading, and when the nurse gently moved away she noticed that they were dozing off peacefully, too.

Hospitals are full of expensive equipment nowadays and it can all do wonderful things, but there will never be any substitute for a nurse with a kind heart.

I CAN'T remember who said, "Anything which helps us to forget ourselves is a blessing."

However, it reminds me of Catherine Booth, granddaughter of the founder of the Salvation Army who claimed she had learned to forget her own problems by entering into those of others.

She wrote, "I cannot explain why weeping with another dries my own tears, but it does; nor why sharing another's load should make me less conscious of my own, but it does; nor putting out my hand to save some one else from stumbling in their sorrow keeps my foot from slipping, but it does . . ."

TIME TO STAND AND STARE

THE FRIENDSHIP BOOK

THE Lady of the House was visiting an elderly friend the other day, when her granddaughter arrived carrying a small bunch of garden flowers. "For you, Gran, from my own garden," she said.

My friend, a devoted churchgoer, thanked her and then added, "Do you know who made them grow, Emma?"

"Oh, yes," answered the child promptly. "God made them grow. But, Gran, I helped them along. I planted the seeds, and weeded the plot, and watered them, just as Daddy showed me."

How right she was! Isn't that exactly what our role is — to help along the things that He has given us?

REJOICE in the Lord alway: and again I say, Rejoice.   Philippians 4,4.

YOU have been trying to do something for a long time without success and are now thinking of giving up? Then don't!

An old legend tells of how the Devil decided to sell some of his tools. One by one they were exhibited and sold. To some people's surprise the one which fetched the highest price was blunt-edged.

When someone asked why this was so, the Devil replied, "Ah, that is my most useful and valuable tool — the tool of discouragement."

Don't let the Devil have his way. You have a stronger force on your side.

AUGUST

DAISIES

*W*HEN I was very, very small —
  A little girl of four,
I used to pick the daisies
  On the lawn outside the door.

I used to choose the biggest ones
  And weave a lovely chain;
The tiny blossoms often shone
  With dewdrops or with rain.

I used to thread the daisies,
  There kneeling in the grass,
While overhead, in beauty,
  The clouds of Summer passed.

Those days were oh, so wonderful,
  Without a single care,
And now I weave sweet memories
  Just sitting in a chair.

Margaret H. Dixon.

A VICAR was leaving to take up duties in another church and his parishioners were giving him a farewell party.

One lady was quite overcome by the occasion and said, "Oh, Vicar, I *am* sorry you are leaving us!"

"Never mind, my dear," the man replied consolingly, "you might get somebody better than me."

The lady burst into tears. "That's just what they said last time!" she sobbed.

THE FRIENDSHIP BOOK

ONE Summer's day the Lady of the House and I were walking along one of the main streets of Oxford when a kitten ran out of a shop straight onto the road. It was struck by a bus and one of its tiny paws must have been injured for when it walked away it was limping.

Suddenly, a taxi pulled up. The driver jumped out and, ignoring the lanes of hooting buses, cars and lorries, gathered the kitten into his arms and, carrying it very gently, walked back to his taxi.

When the Lady of the House congratulated him, he said, "Well, I couldn't leave the poor little creature. I'll take it to the vet and then trace the owner."

I'd intended writing about one of Oxford's eminent sons, but The Lady of the House says that although this story will not go down in history, it is just as important. I'm sure she's right.

ANDREW BROWN has been a qualified solicitor for some years now. When he began his career, he was anxious to make a big impression, and had just got a telephone installed in his office. He tells the story of how he was waiting for his first client when he noticed, through the glass door, a man about to enter.

He grabbed the shiny new receiver and plunged into an imaginary conversation: "Yes, I'll attend to that for you. No, I hadn't forgotten, but this morning I was asked to settle a big damages suit and had to put it off because I was just too busy with other cases, but I'll manage to fit you in somehow. Goodbye."

Thinking how well he must have impressed his visitor, Andrew hung up. "Excuse me, sir," said the man. "I've come to connect your phone."

SATURDAY—AUGUST 5.

ROAD accidents always horrify us and I'm sure we'd all like to play our part in helping to reduce the annual toll of deaths and terrible injuries.

Recommended to the readers of a parish magazine some time ago was this Driver's Prayer which I'd like to pass on:

> *God grant me a careful hand*
> *And watchful eye,*
> *That no one may be hurt*
> *When I go by.*

SUNDAY—AUGUST 6.

NOW thanks be unto God, which always causeth us to triumph in Christ, and maketh manifest the savour of his knowledge by us in every place.

Corinthians II 2,14.

MONDAY—AUGUST 7.

LAST autumn we went to visit a young doctor friend, Andrew, who lives in Perth, Scotland. He has a little daughter, Penelope, and when we visit them, she likes the Lady of the House to hear her prayers and tuck her in at bedtime.

This time Penelope managed to say The Lord's Prayer on her own. "Thy Kingdom come, Thy will be done in Perth as it is in heaven," she whispered.

When The Lady of the House came downstairs and told us, we laughed, but later, as we were talking about it, we decided she was quite right. It was as important for His will to be done in Perth as in any other place. Don't you agree?

H

THE FRIENDSHIP BOOK

OUR young friend Paul was telling me about his first climb recently. He was very proud that though he is only eight years old, he had stood on top of a hill a thousand feet high, right above the little Aberdeenshire village where he was spending a holiday.

"I saw *everything,* Mr Gay," he said. "Every single house in the village stood out. It all looks different when you're up above like that, doesn't it?"

I think that when Paul grows up he will find that not only villages, but men and women, too, look different when you see them from another viewpoint. So many quarrels would not take place, so many harsh judgments would be avoided if, like young Paul, we could stand back — as if on a hilltop — and view the whole picture.

OLDER readers may remember the days when street lamps were lit by the lamplighter with a little flame on a long pole.

C. H. Spurgeon, the well-known Baptist preacher, was once walking home with a friend after an evening service when he noticed, away ahead, a lamplighter busy at work.

"Did you see that?" said Spurgeon to his friend.

"See what?" was the reply.

"Why, those lamps coming on one by one behind the man carrying his little light on a pole." As Spurgeon was speaking, the lamplighter disappeared over the brow of the hill.

"There," said the preacher, "that's what I would like to do. I would like to leave lighted lamps behind me when I go over the hill and am seen no more."

Not a bad ambition for any of us, I think.

THE FRIENDSHIP BOOK

DURING a walking holiday in the Malvern Hills, the Lady of the House and I made a special point of visiting Little Malvern.

We wanted to see the home, for the last ten years of her life, of the Stockholm-born opera singer, Jenny Lind, often called "the Swedish Nightingale". We had to ask our way and were directed to Wynd's Point by an old man who was steeped in the history of the town.

He told us an interesting story about Jenny Lind. She had retired from singing before she settled in Malvern, but she did in fact give a final performance there. A railway porter carrying her luggage at the station one day very timidly asked her if she would consider singing at a concert in aid of the Railwaymen's Benevolent Fund. To his delight and surprise, she agreed. And so her last public performance was not in a great opera house, but in a village hall.

MRS VIOLET BARNETT of Pinxton in the Midlands had only a small garden but it was outstanding enough to have gained itself a place in a television gardening programme. The garden was devoted entirely to roses and showed a kind of "family tree" of their development over the years.

"This is really marvellous," the interviewer said, "but having only roses, doesn't your garden seem very barren and colourless during the Winter?"

"Oh, that doesn't bother me one bit," she replied. "You see, I know what's going to come in the Summer."

Well, they do say gardeners make the best philosophers!

THE FRIENDSHIP BOOK

THE other evening a group of us were having a rather depressing conversation — or at least we were listening to a rather depressing monologue by a mutual acquaintance who was riding his favourite hobby horse of "What's wrong with the world".

Eventually, my friend Herbert broke in, "Well, you're right of course, Arnold. There are *hundreds* of things wrong with the world, but I'll tell you this — for every one thing you tell me that's wrong with the world, I'll tell you two that are right with it!"

BELOVED, let us love one another; for love is of God; and every one that loveth is born of God, and knoweth God.   John I 4,7.

"MARRIAGE LINES" is the title of this thoughtful poem by Chrissy Greenslade:

> The first year of a marriage
>   Holds excitement, joy and love,
> The bond you share together,
>   Linked with help from God above.
> Each step you take in harmony
>   Makes strong the threads you weave,
> Your faith and pleasure growing
>   As you trust and not deceive.
> Companionship and friendship
>   Will develop through the years,
> And you will find life's pathway
>   Filled with happiness, not tears.

BENEATH BLUE SKIES

TUESDAY—AUGUST 15.

AS a young man John felt called to the mission field — there was never a doubt in his mind about what he wanted to do. After a lengthy training, he was accepted by a missionary society and around the same time he met and married a girl as eager to serve others as himself. It was therefore a very happy and confident man who sailed for India with his bride.

They had three children who flourished, as did their ministry, but for some reason John's wife became unsettled and began to yearn for home.

Eventually she became ill and the entire family was forced to return to England. Here her health improved, but she steadfastly refused to live abroad again. John felt upset and frustrated, worried about his wife and defeated in his career. You see, he'd been so sure of his calling.

That was half a century ago. Due to the circumstances of his life, he was to remain in England, but in time, each one of his three children felt called to the mission field themselves. In his later years, John found great peace for it was as if his own destiny had been fulfilled through his children.

"I never attempted to influence them," he would say, "but I often find comfort in the knowledge that for the two who returned, three have gone back to service overseas . . ."

WEDNESDAY—AUGUST 16.

I CAME across this choice comment the other day: "The real art of conversation is not only to say the right thing in the right place, but to leave unsaid the wrong thing at the tempting moment."

I don't know the author, but the words make sense, don't they?

THE FRIENDSHIP BOOK

THE Lady of the House and I attended a jumble sale recently, and were interested to find an album into which had been pasted favourite pictures and cuttings, including this verse:

Jesus is coming! — It might be today
So don't say the things you would normally say,
Those angry words, would you like Him to hear?
Would you sit and waste time when there's work
  you could do
If you knew that the Saviour was looking at you?
If you knew that today when the clock had struck
  four
The Saviour Himself would be there at your door,
Would you still be unwashed, your sink full to the
  brim?
Or would you be ready and waiting for Him?
Would your things be untidy or all put away,
If you knew He was coming for certain today?

I HEARD recently of someone who founded a Society for the Abolition of Nursery Rhymes! He maintained that they put the wrong ideas into children's heads. Little Boy Blue, fast asleep in the hay, encouraged laziness; the Knave of Hearts, thieving; Jack Horner in his corner with his pie, greed; Goosey, Goosey Gander, with the old man being thrown downstairs, cruelty.

I confess to being more amused than shocked when I read all this, but doesn't it just show how we can find bad in anything if we are determined to seek it out? How much better to look for the good in circumstances and in people.

JUST THINK...

When rocks were riven long ago,
Dividing sea and land,
Primeval man his footprint marked
With wonder on the sand —
And still we find enchantment there
Along the golden strand.

THE FRIENDSHIP BOOK

SATURDAY—AUGUST 19.

WHAT do you say when you write a letter of sympathy to someone who has suffered a bereavement? Well, there's no easy answer, but really, it doesn't matter what you say.

If you're thinking of writing — then go ahead at once! Don't be put off because you feel awkward and words don't come easily.

I couldn't count the number of times people who have suffered a bereavement have described the comfort and support they have found in letters from friends and sometimes, too, from casual acquaintances they would never have expected to hear from.

So, if you're merely *thinking* of writing, then go ahead and do it! Only when we're suffering the heartache of bereavement can we really understand how much a few sincere sentences can mean.

SUNDAY—AUGUST 20.

HUMBLE yourselves in the sight of the Lord, and he shall lift you up.   James 4,10.

MONDAY—AUGUST 21.

WHENEVER I eat figs I think about my friends! Why? Well, there is something unusual about fig trees — they never have blossom on their branches. The flowers are inside the fruit which is why figs are so full of seeds.

New acquaintances are often like these figs. They often have so much inside them which, given time, will blossom forth. I have seen it happen again and again, and I bless them for it.

THE FRIENDSHIP BOOK

I LIKE the title of C. S. Lewis's book, "Surprised by Joy", because it reminds me that the most ordinary day can be filled with glad surprises if we are on the look-out for them.

It is a pity that we seem to reserve the word "surprise" for the more sensational things, whereas, in fact, life is crammed with tiny surprises — the pattern of frost on the window pane on a cold morning, an unexpected letter or visit from a friend, a book by a writer hitherto unknown, a sudden shaft of sunlight which brightens a dark corner, a blackbird's song, the smile of a little child, an encouraging word spoken to us. Surprise! Surprise! How true is the saying, "I come in the little things, saith the Lord."

ON the occasions when we feel dejected and of no use to ourselves or anyone else, it can be very helpful to try to look outwards until we are able to see things in perspective again.

I think Dr William Barclay expressed that thought very well in this prayer:

"When I feel that I am useless and a burden to others, help me to remember that I can still pray, and so help me constantly to uphold the hands of those I love, and constantly to bear them and myself to your throne of grace."

On the same theme, there is one of the Lady of the House's favourite quotations:

"I was sorry that I had no shoes until I saw a man without any feet."

Sometimes we're so immersed in our own apparently all-consuming troubles that it takes a real effort to realise there are many far worse off than us.

THE FRIENDSHIP BOOK

A LOCAL church has established quite a reputation for itself with its simple but striking Wayside Pulpit posters. Many people, among them a good number who do not go to any church, have told me how much they look forward to seeing the weekly message.

I am sure this one will have struck many people by its directness and simplicity: "Life is precious; handle it with prayer."

A LADY'S watch had been left on a pew after a service. The following Sunday the Vicar announced that it was in his possession and that the owner could claim it afterwards.

Concluding the notices he said, "We will now sing hymn number 267, 'Lord, her watch, thy Church is keeping'."

I N this verse, the Bolton poet, Phyllis Ellison, tells us why it's better to smile than to frown:

> *Frowns make wrinkles on your face,*
> *Smiles put crinkles in their place;*
> *There's not much difference*
> *Between the two,*
> *But laughter lines*
> *Are better for you.*
> *So if you have wrinkles,*
> *Smooth them out with a smile,*
> *You'll find that a crinkle*
> *Is more worthwhile.*

GOOD COMPANY

It's nice to be independent
  With a place to call your own,
And someone to share the friendship there,
  More fun than being alone.

THE FRIENDSHIP BOOK

FOR ye are all the children of God by faith in Christ Jesus.

Galatians 3,26.

IN earlier days of BBC broadcasting, Sir Eric Geddes told listeners, "Life's more like a tree than a ladder. It branches in different directions, not directly upwards by rungs.

"Sometimes," he added, "we have to re-start life on a new branch to move upwards."

This is all too true and we only have to reflect a moment to quote Sir Winston Churchill who started on the wrong branch of life's tree as a soldier. Even his second branch — politics — was shaky before 1939, and only his authorship branch remained stable. Yet he was to become a world-famous leader and one of the greatest men in history.

Conan Doyle was a doctor of medicine before becoming an author as was A. J. Cronin.

Sir Henry Royce of Rolls-Royce fame had a restricted education and little money. There seemed little potential for his later fame, when at 10 years old he was delivering papers, before becoming a telegram boy. Then aged 17, he switched to another branch of life's tree. He went to work in a tool factory toiling 54 hours a week for a few shillings. However, he worked and studied the new motoring era and went on to build a great business renowned throughout the world.

These great men found fulfilment in a new and challenging area of life. Even if they had not succeeded, they would still have had the satisfaction that they had tried hard!

THE FRIENDSHIP BOOK

I WONDER if you know this old Sanskrit verse which expresses a beautiful thought in just a few simple lines:

> Look well to this day.
> Yesterday is but a dream
> And tomorrow is only a vision,
> But today well-lived
> Makes every yesterday a dream of happiness
> And every tomorrow a vision of hope.
> Look well therefore to this day.

"HOW old are you, Granny?" asked little Tom as he had tea with her in her country cottage.

"Oh, you should never ask a lady her age!" said Granny, passing a plate of freshly-made cakes. "But I'll tell you. I'll be ninety-six next month."

"Ninety-six?" breathed the little boy in hushed tones. "Have you lived in this village all your life, then?"

"No," smiled Granny, "not yet!"

OF course it's good that we should go to church, but we should never forget that there's more to being a Christian than regular attendance every Sunday. Morris Abel Bear put it like this:

> Who builds a church within his heart
>   And takes it with him everywhere
> Is holier far than he whose church
>   Is but a one-day house of prayer.

SEPTEMBER

FRIDAY—SEPTEMBER 1.

I SUPPOSE our churches never look more beautiful than they do at Harvest Thanksgiving Services when they are decorated with greenery, fruit, flowers, vegetables and sheaves of corn.

Usually there is a central feature in these displays, and I have been interested over the years to notice, in different places, what this is.

Often it is a loaf of bread, "the staff of life", sometimes baked in decorative form, say, as a sheaf of wheat. Sometimes it is an actual sheaf. I have been impressed, too, when at the centre of the display there has simply been set a glass of water.

One I liked particularly, in a village country church which the Lady of the House and I once visited, was a plough. The preacher made this the focus of his sermon, pointing out that every harvest was, so to speak, the joint production of the Providence of God and the labours of man:

> *We plough the fields and scatter*
> *The good seed on the land,*
> *But it is fed and watered*
> *By God's almighty hand.*

A co-operation of the human and the divine which is worth remembering, not just at harvest-time, but throughout our lives.

SATURDAY—SEPTEMBER 2.

I LIKE a Chinese proverb which was brought to my notice the other day. It says: "Govern a family as you would cook a small fish — very gently".

BRIGHT MORNING

THE FRIENDSHIP BOOK

LET Your light so shine before men, that they may see your good works, and glorify your Father which is in heaven.   Matthew 5,16.

THE 4th September 1989 marks the 80th anniversary of the first Boy Scout Rally at the Crystal Palace in London, when 11,000 boys marched proudly past their founder, General Sir Robert Baden-Powell.

The Scout Movement has enriched the lives of millions of boys with its emphasis on "Peace, Friendship and Goodwill". Powell aimed to make happy, healthy and helpful citizens and one of the early mottoes based on the scout law was, "A good turn done, a new friend won."

The Chief Scout, as he was known, was a popular figure, admired by scouts all over the world. Truly, as Abraham Lincoln once said, "A man is never so tall as when he stoops to help a child."

THREE boys were once discussing what their fathers did. The first one said, "My father puts together a few words that rhyme, calls it poetry and gets £20 for it."

The second one said, "My father puts a few pieces of wood together, calls it a piece of sculpture and gets £50 for it."

"That's nothing," said the third boy. "My father writes a few notes, calls it a sermon and it takes four men to carry in the money!"

K

THE FRIENDSHIP BOOK

IT is essential to learn how to use knowledge in the right way.

The Physic Garden in Chelsea, begun in 1673 for the study of plants used in medicine, still stands in the same place today. It is used by doctors, pharmacists and lecturers throughout the world.

In its early days, the herbs were heaped together without order. However, when Phillip Miller, the son of a London market gardener, was appointed curator in 1772 he catalogued them and was responsible for a great many other introductions. He was a Scotsman by descent and would not employ a gardener unless he was Scottish!

This "Prince of Gardeners" published books, too, his most famous being a "Gardener's Dictionary" which went into eight editions. Many friends from overseas came to visit him and he let them take away cuttings from Chelsea.

Phillip Miller remained in charge of his Physic Garden until he was 79, having helped to make it as the public see it today. He knew how to use knowledge in the right way, and this is something well worth keeping in mind in these days of advanced technology.

THERE was a time when house-blessings or door-blessings on cards or plaques were common, not only on inns but on private houses, too.

An old one I liked went like this:

> *Hail, Guest! We ask not what thou art:*
> *If Friend, we greet thee, hand and heart;*
> *If Stranger, such no longer be;*
> *If Foe, our love shall conquer thee.*

THE FRIENDSHIP BOOK

YEARS ago in a quiet farmhouse in Wisconsin, USA, a boy lay on his bed enjoying the sight of a glorious sunset. He was suffering from poliomyelitis and earlier that evening he had overheard the doctor downstairs tell his mother that he would be dead by the morning.

The boy made so much fuss about having the furniture in his bedroom moved that his mother thought he was delirious. In fact, all the youngster wanted was to make sure he could see out of the window. If he was going to die before morning, he was determined to see the sunset without having anything to block his view.

The boy's name was Milton Erickson, and he didn't, in fact, die that night. He lived on to become a world-famous psychiatrist and hypnotherapist, and he died in March, 1980 in his late seventies.

One of the many things Dr Erickson taught his patients and students was to try always to have some short-term goal, something to look forward to in the near future, just as when he had looked forward to watching what he thought was going to be his last sunset.

TWO ministers were travelling in the West Highlands. While crossing a loch in a boat with several other passengers, a dreadful storm blew up and one of the passengers was heard to shout, "Those two ministers should start praying or we'll all be drowned!"

"No, no," replied a boatman. "The little one can pray if he likes — but the big one would do better to take an oar!"

PRECIOUS MOMENTS

Summer has a laughing face —
Friendships flourish,
Memories are meadow-sweet —
Made to cherish.

Evergreen the happy days
Spent together;
Youthful pleasures gladly shared
Last forever.

THE FRIENDSHIP BOOK

WE that are strong ought to bear the infirmities of the weak, and not to please ourselves.

Romans 15,1.

I MUST say I have a great likeness for old jugs which bear humorous or moral verses. Sometimes they are very much to the point. Here is one I saw the other day:

For every ill beneath the sun
There is a remedy or none.
If there be one, then try to find it.
If there be none, then never mind it.

I READ a magazine article recently in which a man told of his remarkable escape from an accident and said that the experience had given him a new sense of the value and wonder of life. "Every day now," he said, "I feel is bonus time."

"Bonus time"! I like that phrase, and I don't think we need to have had a miraculous escape, or gone through a life-saving operation to experience it.

Whoever we are, whatever our circumstances, just to be alive today is really "bonus time". And then there are all the pleasant "extras" that crop up: an unexpected meeting with a friend; a surprise letter in the post; a much-loved tune being played on the radio; the sudden burst of sunshine on a winter's day that tempts us to a walk.

Let's look for "bonus time" today!

THE FRIENDSHIP BOOK

THIRTY-FOUR seemed too young to "retire", decided Quaker Francis Frith. He had made a modest fortune as partner in a Liverpool grocery warehouse at an early age and leaving the hustle and bustle behind seemed an attractive proposition.

What could he do in the years ahead? Several ideas crossed his mind and one, in particular stuck. He would become a photographer.

With cumbersome cameras, glass plates and elementary darkrooms he set out on his travels seeking places and subjects to record in pictures. Some of his journeys were abroad but even more fascinating were his explorations to hundreds of villages, towns and cities in Great Britain. He photographed beauty spots, factories, street scenes, historic monuments, mansions and ordinary people going about their daily lives.

His pictures sold to an eager public as did the postcards his printing and photographic firm marketed after 1894. This photographic pioneer died four years later, but nowadays, the Frith Collection of prints from original photographs and glass plates provide an unusual historical and sociological record of Britain in the 1850 period onwards.

Yet these wonderful scenes would never have existed if Francis Frith had not chosen to take up another career. How true it is that we never know our hidden talents until circumstances force us to channel our energies elsewhere.

I WAS amused to see this notice outside a chapel in the Lake District:

"Please close the door to prevent straying sheep from entering — the woolly kind, of course"!

THE FRIENDSHIP BOOK

MAGGIE, a teacher friend, told me of an exercise she gave her secondary school class which you may like to try. She asked her pupils to make a list of all the attributes they would look for in a best friend. As you would expect, the results produced qualities such as loyalty, optimism, honesty, love, warmth, understanding, selflessness, thoughtfulness, confidentiality, sense of humour, truthfulness, encouragement, patience, sincerity, helpfulness, courtesy, reliability, and so on.

The second part of the exercise was more difficult, and you might like to try it yourself. She asked her pupils to name which of the qualities they thought they themselves possessed.

MARGARET WOOD from Burton-on-Trent sent me this poem entitled "Surprise" which she came across in her church magazine:

> *I dreamt death came the other night,*
> *And Heaven's gate swung wide,*
> *With kindly grace an angel came*
> *To usher me inside.*
>
> *Yet there to my astonishment*
> *Stood folk I'd known on earth;*
> *Some I had judged as quite unfit*
> *Or of but little worth.*
>
> *Indignant words rose to my lips,*
> *But never were set free,*
> *For every face showed stunned surprise:*
> *NO ONE EXPECTED ME!*

THE FRIENDSHIP BOOK

AND now abideth faith, hope, charity, these three; but the greatest of these is charity.

Corinthians I 13,13.

DURING the Second World War, Dr Eduard Benes, exiled President of Czechoslovakia, found refuge in the village of Aston Abbotts in Buckinghamshire. He was warmly and sympathetically welcomed by the local people, and with other members of his government stayed until he was able to return to his own country when peace was declared.

Before he left, he wanted to give the villagers a memento of his stay. What would it be? Then he thought of how he had often seen them standing in all weathers waiting for the bus.

That was it! A bus shelter was built in Aston Abbotts as a very practical thank-you from a very human President.

AT a Sunday School Conference a teacher told how, after a lesson on the Good Samaritan, she asked the class to explain what the parable meant.

A small boy at once replied, "Please, Miss, it means that when we are in trouble other people should help us!"

I wonder how much happiness people miss because, like that little boy, they think in terms of other people helping them instead of what they themselves can do to help others?

THE GENTLE TOUCH

Gently deal with those who answer
To our guiding hand;
Quiet words are more effective
Than the stern command.

Sometimes, when the rein is lightest
Our response is best;
Lead, not drive, to be successful,
That's the vital test.

THE FRIENDSHIP BOOK

FROM the USA comes this inspiring piece known as "The Prayer Of An Unknown Confederate Soldier":

I asked God for strength, that I might achieve,
I was made weak, that I might learn humbly to obey;
I asked for health, that I might do greater things,
I was given infirmity, that I might do better things;
I asked for riches, that I might be happy,
I was given poverty, that I might be wise;
I asked for power, that I might have the praise of men,
I was given weakness, that I might feel the need of
*   God;*
I asked for all things, that I might enjoy life,
I was given life, that I might enjoy all things;
I got nothing that I asked for — but everything I had
*   hoped for.*
Almost despite myself, my unspoken prayers were
*   answered.*
I am among all men, most richly blessed.

AILEEN was telling the Lady of the House and myself about one of her young daughter's favourite sayings. Aileen and her husband were going out one evening and she'd particularly wanted to look her best.

As she was putting the last touch to her make-up Aileen turned to Susan and said, "Now, is there anything else I can do to make myself pretty?"

Perhaps Aileen was looking a little worried at that moment. Anyhow, the little girl replied, "Smile, Mummy!"

So often a smile is the crowning touch, isn't it?

THE FRIENDSHIP BOOK

THE poet Anne French-Cheetham wrote these delightful verses which carry a message for every housewife!

Watch the sky on a Summer's day,
When all the world is bracing.
Watch the sky on a Winter's day,
When all the clouds are chasing.
Watch the sky in Springtime,
When the new buds are all breaking.
Watch the sky in Autumn,
When all the leaves are shaking.

From cold and snow to rain and blow,
To sun and shadow-play,
There's something different to be seen
Each moment of each day.
All this you can stand and watch,
If you just keep on looking
Through the kitchen window,
As you do your family's cooking!

DR HERBERT LOCKYER, evangelist and author of nearly 60 books on religion, was still writing and preaching when he was in his nineties. I like the story of the journalist who interviewed him and asked what was the secret of his longevity. He went to a drawer and took out a little box on the lid of which was written "How to live to be 100". Inside was a card which said, "When you reach 99, be very careful"!

THE FRIENDSHIP BOOK

AND he arose, and rebuked the wind, and said unto the sea, Peace, be still. And the wind ceased, and there was a great calm.   Mark 5,39.

A FRIEND who recently lost her husband tells me that she found great consolation in this anonymous poem:

Perhaps, if we could see
The splendour of the land
To which our loved are called from you and me,
We'd understand.

Perhaps, if we could hear
The welcome they receive
From old familiar voices — all so dear —
We would not grieve.

Perhaps, if we could know
The reason why they went,
We'd smile — and wipe away the tears that flow
And wait content.

I WONDER whether we consider ourselves to be rich or poor? I think the poet, Alexander Smith, may have put this in perspective for many of us.

He wrote, "A man's real possession is his memory. In nothing else is he rich, in nothing else is he poor."

An unusual way, perhaps, of measuring riches and poverty — yet how true!

THE FRIENDSHIP BOOK

IF there was an eleventh commandment, what should it be? I put this question to friends one evening and these were some of their suggestions:

"Thou shalt have patience and perseverence".

"Thou shalt not destroy another's self-respect by scorn or disparagement".

"Thou shalt not judge thy neighbour".

"Thou shalt be kind to humans and animals".

"Thou shalt not be a time-waster".

"Thou shalt be grateful for all God's goodness and men's kindness".

Well, which one do *you* prefer? Or have you one or two of your own?

GROWING old brings problems, I know, and it's not always easy to keep looking on the bright side. Julie Longman, of Edinburgh, expresses the optimistic thoughts of one senior citizen in this delightful poem, "Ageing":

> *My back is painful,*
> *But my eyes are bright;*
> *My fingers are twisted,*
> *But my heart is light.*
>
> *I can still whistle,*
> *I can just sing;*
> *Though I can't do a tap dance*
> *Or a Highland Fling!*
>
> *I think about my eyesight*
> *Rather than my back;*
> *Give thanks for my bookcase*
> *And feel no lack.*

THE FRIENDSHIP BOOK

THERE is a beautiful legend which comes to us from mediaeval times. An aged hermit living in the Egyptian desert planted an olive tree near his cave. He then prayed to God for rain, and it came and watered his olive tree.

He thought that some warm sun to swell its buds would be advisable, so he prayed and the sun shone. However, after a time his small tree began to wilt and the hermit thought that a little frost would help to brace it. He prayed for frost and it came. After that he believed a hot southerly wind would suit his tree and for this he also prayed. The south wind came, blew upon his tree and it died.

Some time later, he visited a fellow hermit and at his door was a flourishing olive tree. He asked how his friend had managed to grow it and the other hermit replied, "I planted it, God blessed it and it grew."

"Ah, brother," replied the first hermit, "I, too, planted an olive tree and when I thought it needed water, I asked God for rain and it came. When I thought that it wanted sun, I asked for this and the sun shone, and when I deemed that it needed strength, I prayed and frost came. God gave me all I demanded for my tree and yet it is dead."

"And, I, my brother," replied the other hermit, "I left my tree in God's hands for He knew what it wanted better than I."

A JEWISH father once complained to a rabbi that his son had forsaken God. "What shall I do?" he asked in desperation.

Back came the instant reply, "Love him more than ever."

OCTOBER

SUNDAY—OCTOBER 1.

FOR me to live is Christ, and to die is gain.
Philippians 1,21.

MONDAY—OCTOBER 2.

I LOVE Autumn days. A poet who really captures the spirit of the season for me is W. H. Carruth who wrote:

> A haze on the far horizon,
>   The infinite, tender sky,
> The ripe, rich tint of the cornfields,
>   And the wild geese sailing high;
> And all over the upland and lowland
>   The charm of the golden rod,
> Some of us call it Autumn,
>   And others call it God.

TUESDAY—OCTOBER 3.

YEARS ago, Harry Lomas kept a little village store in a remote part of Cumberland. He was open six days a week, and often in the evenings he would carry groceries to people who were ill or infirm.

Sunday was a busy day for Harry, too. At a time when public transport was almost non-existent on Sundays, he would tramp miles over the hills to conduct services as a lay-preacher.

Asked once why he added this extra activity to an already full and busy week, he replied, "Because I can't eat my bread alone." He wanted to share his faith with others — and isn't this true of all the good things of life? True enjoyment comes only when we share it.

THE FRIENDSHIP BOOK

THE multi-petalled chrysanthemum with its bright colours and evocative Autumn scent did not appear in Europe until the 18th century, although it was known in China from the 5th century B.C.

There's a nice story about its origin. A young Chinese girl was about to be married and she asked a wise man how long her marriage would last. He told her it would be as long as the number of petals on the flower she wore on her wedding day.

Well, the girl searched everywhere, but she could not find flowers with more than five petals. Then, at last, she found one with 17 and with her hairpin she carefully divided each petal into two and then into two again. This became the first chrysanthemum whose meaning in flower language is "long life and purity".

The Chinese girl and her husband lived together happily for 68 years, the exact number of the chrysanthemum petals. She may have been given wise advice, but I think she deserves full marks for her ingenuity, too!

I WAS listening to a radio talk the other day about a lady who had regained her sight after many years of blindness. She was so thankful to be able to see the miracles of creation again that she kept exclaiming, "How beautiful the grass is! How green it is!" She picked up lovely Autumn leaves and took them home in a box because the sight of them was so precious.

"Why don't people say they are so beautiful?" she said.

It made me realise how much we take for granted, not really noticing things because we see them every day. The world is filled with beautiful sights. Let's take time to look at them!

K

THE FRIENDSHIP BOOK

A COMPANY moved into a new office on the 18th storey of a skyscraper block. The new typing pool had a floor to ceiling window, but none of the girls wanted to sit anywhere near it, despite the management's assurances that the glass was unbreakable and perfectly safe.

That was until the site engineer came on the scene. Without saying anything, he removed his safety helmet and jacket, rushed across the room, and hurled himself bodily at the window. It didn't even shudder.

The girls weren't afraid then, and the management have never had any more problems placing staff near the window, thanks to the man who was prepared to put to the test something for which he had himself been responsible.

WE often hear people suffering from physical ailments and emotional upheavals being advised to stop worrying, because that won't solve anything.

This generalisation about "worrying" really is too simplistic and is not very helpful. People in difficulties have to worry, and indeed must worry, but they must worry constructively to find solutions to their problems. What they mustn't do is to worry negatively by punishing themselves for what has happened and by imagining all sorts of disasters.

As Ralph Waldo Emerson said:

> *Some of your hurts you have cured,*
> *And some of the sharpest you have still*
> *   survived.*
> *But what torments of grief you have endured*
> *For the evils which never arrived.*

L

THE FRIENDSHIP BOOK

AND daily in the temple, and in every house, they ceased not to teach and preach Jesus Christ.

Acts 5,42.

I HAVE just been reading a fascinating book, "Gardens in Time" by John and Ray Oldham. "Men have made gardens ever since they ceased to be nomads and settled along the shores of the great rivers of the world."

They point out that, even before then, they sought out many splendid natural landscapes — near mountains, in deep gorges, by river pools — for their festivals, conferences and dances. Gardens are a very real part of our heritage.

A friend of ours used to say, "I carry gardens in my heart." Memories of them, he meant. If we have a garden of our own, even a window box, or a park nearby, or a stretch of countryside not far away, or even only memories of them, let's try to carry them in our heart today.

I SUPPOSE the Lord's Prayer is one of the most frequently repeated prayers in the world — there can be few of us who do not know it. But sometimes, when I join in saying it, I recall some words I heard in a sermon years ago: "The trouble with the Lord's Prayer is that it is often committed to memory, but all too seldom learned by heart."

That's a thought worth pondering — after which we might well say the prayer again!

THE FRIENDSHIP BOOK

YORKSHIRE pudding is made and enjoyed all over the country nowadays, but it is said — rightly or wrongly — that only a Yorkshire woman knows how to make the perfect pudding.

Two essentials are vigorous beating and a square meat tin of smoking hot dripping. It is cooked so that the outside is crisp and the inside soft and succulent, cut into large squares and served with rich beef gravy.

The story goes that the originator of this delicious pudding was housekeeper to a vicar in the Yorkshire Dales. On Sundays, she put on her best hat then vigorously beat the batter in a bowl. When the church bells stopped ringing, she left the batter to stand and hurried across the road to morning service.

As the last hymn ended, she scurried out of church again, and after a final vigorous beat, the mixture was poured into the hot fat.

By the time the vicar had shaken hands with all his parishioners, the pudding was ready to be placed on the table and eaten, in true Yorkshire fashion, before the main course.

A TEACHER friend was smiling as we met her coming out of school. "It's the infants," she said, when we asked her to tell us the joke. "When you ask them a question you never know what's coming."

"Tell me," she had asked the class, "something you can't do."

After much thought little Joanna had said, "I can't swim without water wings."

"Right," said the teacher. "Now tell me something you *can* do."

Joanna was ready: "I can swim with water wings!"

ADMIRATION

THE FRIENDSHIP BOOK

MY Father's way may twist and turn,
My heart may throb and ache,
But in my soul I'm glad I know
He maketh no mistake.

My cherished plans may go astray,
My hopes may fade away,
But still I'll trust my Lord to lead
For He doth know the way.

Tho' night be dark and it may seem
That day will never break,
I'll pin my faith, my all on Him,
He maketh no mistake.

There's so much now I cannot see,
My eyesight's far too dim;
But come what may, I'll simply trust
And leave it all to Him.

For by and by the mist will lift
And plain it all He'll make,
Through all the way, tho' dark to me,
He made not one mistake.

— A.M. Overton.

I SMILED when the Lady of the House told me this light-hearted story.

A Sussex teacher was marking the homework of a rather slow pupil and he asked the young boy who had helped him with it. "My grandma, sir," he replied at once.

"Well, tell your grandma she has managed two out of ten for this."

THE FRIENDSHIP BOOK

THEN spake Jesus again unto them, saying, I am the light of the world: he that followeth me shall not walk in darkness, but shall have the light of life.

John 8,12.

JONATHAN SWIFT wrote that wonderful book "Gulliver's Travels", which can be read either as a tale for children or a biting satire on the follies of mankind. He was inclined sometimes to be a pessimist, but he did know how much a cheerful outlook could help our physical health, for he once wrote that the best doctors are "Dr Diet, Dr Quiet and Dr Merryman".

As a prescription, it would be hard to beat.

ON TV recently I watched a bowls tournament. Not least among the fascinations were the antics of the players as they ran after their bowls as though attempting to bring them by magic as near to the jack as possible. But I wondered, did the bowlers believe that they really had any influence over the woods once they were out of their hands? I think not.

So, too, with everything we do or say. Once we have spoken or acted, however inappropriately, foolishly, or unkindly, it is too late.

Regretting the past is perhaps one of the most common, but futile habits of human beings. How much more valuable it would be if only we could train ourselves to use our time instead, to plan ahead and devise ways of being more careful in future.

THE FRIENDSHIP BOOK

I 'D fill the world with sunshine,
If I but had my way,
Only a little rain would fall
On this or any day,
Umbrellas would be folded tight,
And neatly put away from sight.

I'd fill the world with kindness,
And never an angry word
Would fall upon the listening ear,
And no untruth be heard,
Children with little friends would run
Playing together in the sun.

I'd fill the world with beauty,
With music and with song,
The lilt of lovely melodies
With voices clear and strong,
And in the morn and afternoon,
God would keep all hearts in tune.

Margaret H. Dixon.

AS I strolled along, enjoying a Sunday afternoon walk, my eye was caught by a beech leaf lying on the pavement. It was a beautiful thing of delicate filigree work for nothing remained except a fine network of veins.

As I held it in my hand, I was reminded of the changing form of the human body. The colour in our cheeks and hair may fade, sight and hearing may be impaired, but the real beauty in us is everlasting. Our love, patience, sympathy and kindness are the things that make up the real person, and they are eternal.

THE FRIENDSHIP BOOK

THE REV. BRIAN HESSION was one of those delightful men who was a fluent writer, gifted broadcaster, and a courageous fighter against cancer. As an RAF padre in his early ministry, he was responsible for the welfare of many young men who had had little contact with a clergyman before, and to many of them he became a close friend and cheerful companion.

One lad had an apparently insatiable urge to steal. He had been expelled from school because of this, and had later been caught thieving at a garage. His entry into the RAF as an apprentice was his last chance to make good and he was desperate to be honest.

Then one day it happened again. He went straight to his friend the padre and sobbed out his confession. He had stolen some tools from the workshop, and now bitterly regretted it.

The padre said little, but asked the lad to bring the stolen tools to him. And the Rev. Hession smuggled them back into the workshop one at a time — and was heartily relieved that no one noticed him!

The young man never stole again.

A NATURE lover once wrote: "If you go stamping through a wood in a hurry you will see little. But sit still and the squirrels will come down the trees and the birds will draw near, and Nature will be alive in every twig, tree and flower."

If we have the opportunity today, be it only in park or garden, let us do just that. However, if we can't, let us remember that wherever we are, moments of quiet reflection can bring untold happiness and peace of mind, giving strength and resolve to face tomorrow.

THE FRIENDSHIP BOOK

AND whatsoever ye shall ask in my name, that will I do, that the Father may be glorified in the Son.

John 14,13.

HERE are some charming lines written by Phyllis Ellison of Bolton:

GIVE ME . . .

— The sun in the morning
To brighten my day,
The moon at night
To light my way,
A word with a friend,
A smile from a stranger,
God's guiding hand
To keep me from danger.

DURING an Evangelical service the minister told the congregation that he would be happy to include a special prayer for anyone who felt that his failings were more than he could cope with. A man called Bob Brown stood up and said that he could not cope with money. He was a spendthrift and wasted his wages on trivia.

"I can't rid myself of the habit of throwing my money away," he complained sadly.

"Thank you for owning up to this grievous fault," said the minister. "We will all pray for Brother Brown. But first let us take up the collection!"

THE FRIENDSHIP BOOK

I SUPPOSE the Eiffel Tower is one of the most famous landmarks in the world. Have you heard of the visitor to Paris who spent day after day sitting at the top of the Tower, and when it was suggested to him that he must be very fond of it, he replied, "Not at all. I sit up here because it's the only place in Paris where you cannot see the thing!"

Even Eiffel himself seemed to tire of it a little. "I really ought to be jealous of the Tower," he once said. "People seem to think it is my only work, but I have done some other things, too."

He had indeed. Those "other things" included bridges, wind tunnels, work on aeroplane wing design, and a light steel frame to support the massive Statue of Liberty in New York harbour.

Many of his engineering ideas were copied all over Europe and when a colleague protested about this to Eiffel, suggesting that more secrecy ought to be exercised with their plans, Gustave Eiffel shrugged off the idea, saying, "I have had the enjoyment of inventing something. Why shouldn't others have the enjoyment of using it? Besides, I can always discover something new!"

I like that. Surely good ideas — even our own — are to be shared, not jealously guarded.

I HAVE often shared with you the thoughts I have seen on the Wayside Pulpit of one of our local churches — those brief, simple sayings which are often so very striking and full of meaning.

Here is one which struck me forcibly recently: "The times when it seems hardest to pray are the times when we ought to pray hardest."

THE FRIENDSHIP BOOK

ONE of the pages of my old autograph album has this anonymous verse:

Art thou lonely, O my brother?
Share thy little with another!
Stretch a hand to one unfriended,
And thy loneliness is ended.

Not great poetry, perhaps, but quite a thought.

FEW people have been more gifted than Kathleen Ferrier. She was pretty, an accomplished pianist, had an infectious sense of fun and, of course, a wonderful contralto voice known all over the world.

Her voice was known to millions. At Carlisle Festival, after winning the piano medal, a friend bet her a shilling she wouldn't go in for the contralto singing section. Kathleen never refused a dare. She was amazed when she not only won the section, but walked off with the Rose Bowl for being the outstanding singer there. The judge advised her to take up singing as a career. She did, and won worldwide acclaim.

For the last few years before her tragically short life ended, Kathleen knew she had cancer. However, she never lost her irrepressible sense of humour, and despite operations and long spells of treatment, her singing was never better than in her last months.

After her death, a close friend said, "There was too much jollity in her for us to remember her with sadness. Great as she was as a singer, she was greater still as Kathleen Ferrier."

A wonderful tribute — and one we can all achieve, no matter how much or how little fame we attain.

THE FRIENDSHIP BOOK

AND as ye would that men should do to you, do ye also to them likewise.

Luke 6,31.

OUR friend Annie has worked hard all her life. She does not have good health and has had her share of ups and down which she never talks about.

When The Lady of the House had a nasty cold, Annie was the first person to offer help with our shopping. She is forever going out of her way to cheer others, visiting the sick in hospital and bringing comfort to those with sore hearts.

The secret of all this activity, she once confided to me, is her faith, and then she added thoughtfully, "Doing nothing is such a tiring thing, because it's impossible to stop to take a rest!"

WHEN the New English Bible was being prepared some 30 years ago, the committee responsible tried to find a more modern version of the words "the fatted calf" in the parable of the Prodigal Son.

The chairman made a list of possible substitutes and then took it along to Smithfield Market, and asked the men there which they would use to describe an animal about to be slaughtered.

One of the workers read the list carefully, and shook his head. "We wouldn't say any o' these," he said. "You see, we've got technical terms — we would call 'em fatted calves!"

NOVEMBER

WEDNESDAY—NOVEMBER 1.

CAN'T you almost hear the wind in this fine poem,
"The Intruder", by Anne French-Cheetham?

It comes upon a Winter's night, this bandit of the air,
Rushing round the skirting-boards and dashing up the
stair.
It roves around the door-jambs in its wild, precarious
fight
To get into the bedrooms and rattle on all night.

It squeezes through the keyholes and scampers from
the door,
Skips and trips around our feet and scurries o'er the
floor.
It will sweep around for hours, not resting for a
minute,
As it makes our home a chilly place — and everybody
in it.

It whistles up the chimney-piece and causes soot to
fall,
Then everybody quickly steps it out into the hall.
Is there nowhere we can shelter, no place that we can
hide,
No way that we can keep this fiend firmly
OUTSIDE?

THURSDAY—NOVEMBER 2.

I WAS amused to read about the notice which was
attached to a faulty washing machine at a Baptist
seminary: "This machine filleth with water, but it
toileth not. Neither doth it spin."

THE FRIENDSHIP BOOK

IN Ilkley's Manor House Museum in Yorkshire is a long seat under one of the ancient windows overlooking the courtyard. A notice states: —

"This seat was found built into a window recess in the house where Thomas Chippendale was born in Otley. It may have been carved by his father who also made furniture in oak, and the wood may possibly be local grown. The entry in the Otley Parish Register reads: —

1718 June 5
Thomas, son of John Chippendale
— Otley Joyner.

Fathers have often given encouragement, perhaps unknowingly, to their children in other ways. Mary Webb, the Shropshire novelist, once stated how much she owed to her father, George Edward Meredith.

"The companionship of such a mind as my father's — a mind stored with old tales and legends that did not come from books, and rich with an abiding love for the beauty of forest and harvest field, all the more intense perhaps because it found little opportunity for expression."

Those very tales and legends were woven into the fabric of Mary Webb's imagination and helped to provide famous novels such as "Precious Bane" and "Gone to Earth". The influence of our parents is often very far reaching indeed as these two examples show.

I COULDN'T help smiling at the slip of paper which someone had stuck on the inside of the window of my railway carriage.

It read: "A ticket examiner is a man who never wants to inspect your ticket until you're asleep."

THE FRIENDSHIP BOOK

THOU art worthy, O Lord, to receive glory and honour and power: for thou hast created all things, and for thy pleasure they are and were created.

Revelation 4,11.

DURING a wet spell I was once feeling a bit under the weather. I had a cold that had been hanging on for weeks and it was beginning to get me down, so when the Lady of the House said finally, "You really must go and see the doctor," I replied, "Well, yes. I have half a mind to."

"No, Francis," was the stern reply, "that won't do. Just put your *whole* mind to it and make an appointment *now!*"

So I did, and the doctor was able to give me a lot of relief. More than that, my good lady's words made me realise how much we can miss in life because we have only half a mind to do something. I think that did me more good even than the cure.

THERE are many things I ponder,
Where and how, and when and why?
And I cannot tell the answers
But I'm certain that one day,
I will understand the reasons
For the pleasures and the pain.
What today is quite a mystery
Tomorrow will be plain.

D.J. Morris.

GRATITUDE

Thank you, God, for waters calm,
For silence, moving as a psalm,
Thank you, God, for Winter sun,
And tranquil heart when day is done.

L

THE FRIENDSHIP BOOK

IN the early 15th century, a certain Brother Thomas sat writing in the Monastery of Mount St Agnes, near Zwolle in The Netherlands. His work was intended to be a help to both himself and his brother monks.

Instead, it became one of the most influential books ever written and indeed, no list of the world's bestsellers would be complete without it. Thomas a Kempis's "The Imitation of Christ" has been translated into dozens of languages. It was revered by such as John Wesley, while Dr Samuel Johnson referred to it often. A favourite quote was: "Be not angry when you cannot make another do as you would have them to be, since you cannot make yourself all you wish to be." How true this is!

The famous novelist George Eliot portrayed Maggie Tulliver's reaction to "The Imitation Of Christ" in her novel, "The Mill on the Floss". Leo Tolstoy also mentions it in "War and Peace", while Charles Kingsley called it "the school of many a noble soul". There can be no doubt of the impact Brother Thomas's work has had over the centuries.

Nowadays, people studying, or even merely dipping into "The Imitation of Christ", often find some memorable gem of wisdom. Here's a point for us to ponder — "How often when we have spoken do we later wish we had kept silent"?

THE best piece of advice I ever heard was that which Pope John I gave to himself. It was good advice, not just for a Pope, but for every parent, friend, teacher, minister and manager — in fact, for everyone. It was this: "See everything, overlook a lot, and correct a little."

M

THE FRIENDSHIP BOOK

JAMES ALFRED EGGAR was a bit bothered when the local branch of the National Farmers' Union proposed to hold a carnival. It was May 1916, and at a time when so many British soldiers had been killed in the Great War, it seemed to him that a carnival was most inappropriate. He suggested a solution to the matter: for two minutes there should be a complete silence in memory of all the men who had died.

This silence was duly observed by 2000 people assembled in Farnham's Castle Street and some years later, after the end of hostilities, Mr Eggar's idea was adopted by the Government and became the Armistice "Silence" which is now observed annually at 11 o'clock on the Sunday nearest to the 11th day of November.

THE story is told of an old Highlander who used to go out every morning and stand for a few minutes with his hat off.

One day, a friend observed him and after the man had replaced his hat, asked if he had been saying his prayers.

With a smile, the Highlander replied, "No, I've come here every morning for years to take off my bonnet to the beauty of the world."

AND unclean spirits, when they saw him, fell down before him, and cried, saying, Thou art the Son of God.   Mark 3,11.

THE FRIENDSHIP BOOK

MONDAY—NOVEMBER 13.

I WAS talking with a very old friend about children's games. He remembered how, when he was a boy in Newcastle-on-Tyne, they played a game called "Show Your Light" or "Show Yor Leet" as they say there.

You needed a dark street — they were common enough when he was a boy — and a cheap bull's eye lantern. The boy with the lantern showed a flash of light and the others had to find him in the dark.

My friend told me how the game had inspired a local poet to write these verses:

> *There's a leet within each breast,*
> *Its name's friendship and a test*
> *Will show it's just the brightest you can find:*
> *Not just in its abode,*
> *But on all to whom bestowed*
> *Its radiance will outshine any other kind.*
>
> *So as you older grow*
> *Do not dowse it — let it glow*
> *And shine it on the Folks in Sorrow Street.*
> *There's plenty you can find*
> *If you only have a mind*
> *And play the noble game, "Jack, show yor leet!"*

TUESDAY—NOVEMBER 14.

A FRIEND sent me this item which appeared originally in a church magazine in Idaho, USA.

A trumpet player in the Salvation Army Band was pleased when a lady gave him a ten dollar bill, but his pleasure evaporated somewhat when she said, "one dollar for the Army and nine dollars for music lessons."

THE FRIENDSHIP BOOK

THESE encouraging lines were written by the poet, Phyllis Ellison:

If we could learn to divide by two,
Half for me and half for you,
All our cares would seem much less,
And greater would be our happiness.
For cares that are shared
Just dwindle and die,
While joys will simply multiply.

THE most hospitable plants in our garden are the teasels. From the time they break ground in the Spring to their downfall in Winter's storms, they are "home" to countless creatures. Insects of all shapes and sizes explore their spiny green heads, sparrows come to drink the water collected in their cupped leaves, and when the first mauve florets appear, bees in great variety besiege them, and there is a constant hovering of butterflies.

After the flowers are over and the garden tidied up for Winter, the teasels are left standing, arid and brown; and, improbable as it may seem, still expecting visitors. On the dreariest of Winter days the new visitors arrive: first one solitary goldfinch flashing its colour about the topmost teasel, and soon more than 20 winging around as they feast on the seeds and fill the garden with their radiance, until it seems Summer has come back again. Every year they come, and we always watch for them. The Lady of the House calls it "The Afterglow".

It's surprising how often, when things are at their bleakest, we can find an afterglow — if we watch out for it.

THE FRIENDSHIP BOOK

A FRIEND of ours, a member of the local church, is one of the busiest people I know. She serves on a multitude of committees and is always ready to help anyone in need, as well as meeting the demands of a young family. I happen to know, too, that she spends quite a while early each day in prayer and Bible study.

I once said to her, "Amy, I don't know how you find time for all the things you do."

"Oh, Francis," she replied, "you can never *find* time to do all the things you want. It's a case of *making* time — snatching it out of all the hubbub of the day for the things one feels are most important."

I now feel I know something of the secret of busy, yet calm people.

M Y thanks to Hazel Aitken who sent me this verse describing an experience we have all felt at one time or another:

> *I didn't really have the time*
> *To knock upon her door;*
> *To sit and listen whilst she*
> *Told me tales I'd heard before.*
> *I didn't think I had the time*
> *To step out of my way,*
> *But I'm so glad I MADE the time*
> *To cheer her lonely day.*

B UT lay up for yourselves treasures in heaven, where neither moth nor rust doth corrupt, and where thieves do not break through nor steal.

Matthew 7,20.

THE FRIENDSHIP BOOK

WHEN the Lady of the House came in the other afternoon, she was looking thoughtful. She'd been having tea with our old friends, Lewis and Helen.

"You know," she began, "how keen Helen is on her china collection? And how she never uses any of it?"

I nodded.

"Well . . ." She paused dramatically. "Lewis said he'd make us a cup of tea, and he deliberately set the table with Helen's precious cups and saucers from the china cabinet! She was horrified and asked him what on earth he was doing. And do you know what he replied?"

"I can't imagine," I said.

"Well, he said, 'I just thought that for once we should give these objects the chance to fulfil their purpose'," my wife replied slowly. Then she added, "It made me think, Francis. Can you imagine anything worse than never, in your life, having been of use to anybody?"

We pondered over that together. Something indeed to be avoided, surely!

IN his "Table Talk", Martin Luther makes this odd remark: "When I am assailed with heavy tribulation, I rush out among my pigs rather than remain alone by myself."

What he meant, of course, was that one of the best antidotes to our own troubles is activity, to *do* something, not just to sit and brood. Best of all, if we can do something for somebody less fortunate than ourselves, we'll have found one of the surest ways of distracting our attention from our own worries.

THE FRIENDSHIP BOOK

"YOU can't judge a book by its cover" is a statement which is often shown to be true and I was reminded of it on reading Fred Lemon's autobiography. When he was quite young, he drifted into a life of crime which became more and more serious until he ended up serving a long prison sentence. During this time he became a Christian, which changed his whole attitude to life.

After his release he became a popular speaker and one of the stories he liked to tell is about a prison concert in Dartmoor which was attended by a titled lady.

The Governor was pointing out the members of the orchestra, dressed for the occasion in dinner jackets and bow ties. "That violinist, he's doing five years for robbery . . . the cellist is a forger . . ." and so on.

The lady looked interested. "And the pianist, what did he do?" she asked. "He looks a real villain."

"Well, actually, he's our Chaplain," replied the Governor.

I KNOW we cannot live in the past alone, yet when I ponder some of the wise sayings of people long ago I cannot help feeling how up-to-date many of them are and how much we have to learn from them still.

Terence was a Roman poet and playwright who lived in the second century B.C. and we can still benefit from these words of his: "There is nothing so easy but that it becomes difficult when you do it with reluctance, and nothing so difficult but that it becomes easy when you do it with eagerness."

FRIDAY—NOVEMBER 24.

WAY back in 1757, William Skenelsby pushed a loaded wheelbarrow up the High Street of Pinner in Middlesex for a youth who hadn't the strength to manage it himself.

William was a mere 100 years old when he rendered that good deed for the day, and he lived another 18 years after that, according to his memorial in Pinner Churchyard.

He had spent all his life in service with different households, and probably never thought himself very important. Yet here am I, over two centuries later, remembering him, not for the great age he reached, but for his willing hands and heart.

SATURDAY—NOVEMBER 25.

I USED sometimes to pass along a rather gloomy street, and it was never more so than on a dark Winter's night. However, on certain evenings a service would be in progress in a church halfway along and the lights shining through the stained-glass windows looked almost magical, transforming the whole scene.

It reminded me of some words of Elisabeth Kubler-Ross in her book, *To Live And To Die:*

"People are like stained-glass windows; they sparkle and shine when the sun is out, but when the darkness sets in, their true beauty is only revealed if there is light from within."

SUNDAY—NOVEMBER 26.

FOR every house is builded by some man; but he that built all things is God.   Hebrews 3,4.

GOLDEN MOMENTS

THE FRIENDSHIP BOOK

MRS E. J. Allen of West Horsley, Surrey, sent me a poem which brightened my day. I hope it does the same for you.

> *Perhaps this thought may cheer you:*
> *If, at any time of day,*
> *You're feeling sad and lonely,*
> *And God seems far away—*
> *Fling open wide your window,*
> *Or take a walk outside,*
> *And look right up above you*
> *Where fleecy, white clouds ride.*
> *A God, who paints the heavens*
> *For man's pure sheer delight,*
> *Is not the God to leave you*
> *Alone to bear the fight.*
> *Remember, when you're lonely,*
> *The sky is always fair;*
> *And just behind the canvas*
> *Dwells One who knows your care.*

IN the 18th century, a quiet gentleman often used to walk around Bradford, especially in the poorer areas. He kept his hands clasped behind his back, and they were full of pennies. In those days a penny could buy quite a lot and poor folk, including the children, knew that they were welcome to help themselves and take one or two of the coins. As the recipients of his gifts were behind him, he did not know who had accepted his money.

What a wonderful way of being helpful! Too often, kind deeds are spoiled by the way they are carried out. Abraham Sharp made sure that those receiving his gifts suffered no embarrassment.

THE FRIENDSHIP BOOK

WILLIAM BOOTH, the founder of the Salvation Army, was a giant of evangelism, both in quality and in stature.

His movement grew quickly for he was concerned with both the physical and spiritual needs of the people he worked amongst in the East End of London. He once said, "It is impossible to comfort men's hearts with the love of God when their feet are perishing with cold."

He drove himself hard and expected no less of his "Army". He wanted "Godly, go-ahead daredevils". His terse instructions to one of his members was, "Make your will, pack your bag, kiss your girl and be ready in a week."

When he was 83 and almost blind he made his last public speech in London's Albert Hall. He said then:

"While women weep as they do now, I'll fight; while little children go hungry as they do now, I'll fight; while men go to prison, in and out, I'll fight; while there yet remains one dark soul without the light of God, I'll fight — I'll fight to the very end."

WE hear a lot nowadays about the power of mind over matter, but it's not a new idea. Over 100 years ago, the American poet Ella Wheeler Wilcox wrote these lines:

Say you are well, or all is well with you,
And God shall hear your words and make them true.

And hundreds of years before, the writer of the Book of Proverbs in the Bible said, "As a man thinketh in his heart, so he is."

DECEMBER

FRIDAY—DECEMBER 1.

WE all enjoy receiving presents and usually it is the thought that has gone into them that is appreciated as much as the value.

There is something we may give to others which gives pleasure, but costs nothing. It takes only a moment to hand over, but sometimes the memory lasts forever. It enriches the person who receives it without making poorer the one who gives. It creates happiness in the home and goodwill in everyday encounters. It brings sunshine to the sad and cheer to those who are discouraged. Some people are too tired to give one, so give them one of yours, for nobody needs one as much as the person who has no more to give.

What is this amazing gift? Why, a smile!

SATURDAY—DECEMBER 2.

WE can't succeed in everything. We all know what it is to fail at some time or other. It's how we react to failure that counts:

> *What is failure? It's only a spur*
> *To a man who receives it right,*
> *And it makes the spirit within him stir*
> *To go in once more and fight.*
> *If you never have failed, it's an easy guess*
> *You never have known a high success.*

SUNDAY—DECEMBER 3.

AND being made perfect, he became the author of eternal salvation unto all them that obey him.

Hebrews 5:9

THE FRIENDSHIP BOOK

S T. MARY'S PARISH CHURCH, tucked away behind Newgate and the Bank and not far from Barnard Castle's ancient Market Cross, has this beautiful greeting on its inner door:

> No Man Entering a Home Ignores
>   Him who dwells there.
> This is the House of God
>   And He is Here.
> Pray then to Him who loves you
>   And Bids you welcome.
>   Give Thanks
> For those who in years past
> Built this Place to His Glory.
>   Rejoice
> In his gifts of Beauty
> In Art and Music
> Architecture and Handicrafts
>   And Worship Him
> The One God, Father
>   of us all,
> Through Our Lord and Saviour
>   Jesus Christ. Amen.

T HE French entertainer, the late Maurice Chevalier, was a man with a great zest for work and for life who, in his eighties, was still travelling across the world with his famous one-man show.

Asked once about the secret of his vitality and his love of life he said, "Yesterday is to learn from; today is to live in; tomorrow is to plan for."

Who wouldn't enjoy life with a philosophy like that?

THE FRIENDSHIP BOOK

"I AM getting on with my little book," wrote a middle-aged lady on 6th December 1876. The idea for the "little book" had been in her mind since 1871 when she had begun to take an interest in the welfare of the cab-horses she watched from her window.

Her name was Anna Sewell, and the book she was writing was "Black Beauty", which, when it was published, was judged as being "quite a nice story, but unlikely to have a large circulation."

How wrong that critic was! "Black Beauty" is still a children's favourite, selling steadily in many countries of the world.

Anna had no thought of fame when she wrote the book. She just wanted to tell the story of two horses, and some of the dreadful things that happened to them, as a plea for greater kindness to animals. It worked, too, for as a result of "Black Beauty" much of the cruel treatment meted out to horses at that time was stamped out.

THOMAS CARLYLE, the great Scottish writer of last century, had a famous meeting with Auguste Comte, a noted French thinker. When Comte told Carlyle he was going to found a new religion which would sweep away Christianity, Carlyle's reply was:

"Splendid! All you need to do is to speak as no man ever spoke before, to live as no other man ever lived, to be crucified, to rise again on the third day and convince the world you are still alive. Then perhaps men and women will accept your religion."

I can't tell you what the Frenchman said to that, but I have never heard of his great new religion!

THE FRIENDSHIP BOOK

ABRAHAM LINCOLN, the great American president, was a strong believer in prayer.

A friend once asked him how he could afford to spend so much time doing this. Lincoln replied, "I would be the greatest fool on earth if I thought that I could sustain the demands of this high office without the help of a strength which is far greater than my own."

THE Lady of the House and I were talking about the results of an essay competition for children. The winning essays were published in a local paper.

"Just listen to this," she said, and started to read the work of an eleven-year-old. He said that he would like to be a long-distance lorry driver because he would see different countries. He knew there would be problems, however. If he got married and had children and did his duty by his family how could he still do his job properly?

He ended: "I will stop here because I don't know the answer."

Well, we hope he solves his problem. At the same time we couldn't help thinking that if more of us were occasionally willing to admit we didn't know the answer, life would run a lot more smoothly.

FOR now we live, if ye stand fast in the Lord.
Thessalonians I 3,8.

THE FRIENDSHIP BOOK

WHEN Christmas is upon us, we are all apt to leave everything to the last moment, including writing our Christmas cards. However, one would not wish to be as unfortunate as the lady who, last year, to beat the clock bought a box of 20 identical cards because she particularly liked the picture on the front.

In haste, she rushed to write her greetings and stamped and posted 19 of them. The following day she opened the remaining card to look at it closely. You can imagine how she felt when she read the message inside — *This card is just to say that a small present is on its way!*

THE Berkshire poet Phyllis Birchall sums up in this verse the feelings many people have about their church:

A place that you can enter,
A place where you can pray,
A place where you can ease
The burden of a heavy day.
In quietness and solitude,
You feel that God is there,
He'll never turn away from you,
Your troubles he will share.
He will not make life easy,
He does not work that way,
But he will give the strength you need
To meet another day.
So if your cares are many,
The church is there for you,
Just step inside and pray,
And God will show you what to do.

DAY OF WONDER

THE FRIENDSHIP BOOK

A FRIEND of mine who had been with a large company for many years was invited to attend a series of talks for those about to retire.

One of the speakers, who had herself been retired for some time, gave this advice. "When I was nearing retirement, I worried about how my financial situation would change. Would I have enough to live on? It's a practical and natural concern, after all.

"Now that I've been retired for a good while, I know that it's important to invest in the three C's in order to get a good return."

What were these three C's?

Concern for others to keep us from thinking about our aches and troubles too much.

Curiosity about the world to keep us feeling young. Even the wisest can learn a little more every day.

Cheerfulness. It's easier to like yourself when you're cheerful. Remember, other people are like ourselves — they find cheerful people good company. It's the old adage: laugh and the world laughs with you, cry and you cry alone.

Of course, there's no need to wait until retirement to start practising the speaker's words of wisdom. Each and every one of us could benefit from putting her advice into action — today.

T HE other day little Billy stopped me as I came out of the house and asked, "Do you want to know a cure for a headache, Mr Gay?"

"Yes, that might be useful, Billy," I replied.

Quick as lightning came the reply, "Just stick your head through the window and the 'pane' will be gone!"

FRIDAY—DECEMBER 15.

I LIKE this prayer by the late Dr William Barclay which I came across recently:

"I thank you for my friends, for those who understand me better than I understand myself, for those who know me at my worst and still like me, for those who have forgiven me when I had no right to expect to be forgiven. Help me to be as true to my friends as I would wish them to be to me."

SATURDAY—DECEMBER 16.

A CHRISTMAS card last year bore the following inscription:

Thank you, God, is all I can say,
For letting me help in some small way.

Included was a five pound note to be used for someone in need at Christmas.

The lady who sent the money had lost her husband in an accident at work and her first Christmas without him was going to be extremely difficult. However, she was determined that she wasn't going to stay at home and feel sorry for herself, so she helped to prepare a Christmas dinner for the disabled and on Christmas Day she visited a few folk who live alone and get very few visitors.

She had a really happy Christmas because she wasn't thinking only of herself. And that's the true Christmas spirit.

SUNDAY—DECEMBER 17.

B UT the manifestation of the Spirit is given to every man to profit withal.   Corinthians 1 12:7

THE FRIENDSHIP BOOK

THIS delightful poem, "Kindness", is by Margaret H. Dixon of Surrey, and I'm sure readers will agree with the sentiments she expresses so well in these five verses:

> Kindness is a little star,
>   That twinkles in the night,
> Kindness is a little flower,
>   That blossoms out of sight.
>
> Kindness is a loving word,
>   That no one else can hear,
> Kindness is a little song,
>   That brings a world of cheer.
>
> Kindness is a friendly face,
>   When one is growing old,
> Kindness is a glowing warmth,
>   When all the world is cold.
>
> Kindness is a helping hand,
>   Across a busy street,
> Kindness is the loving smile,
>   Which makes our joy complete.
>
> Kindness is a "something"
>   We never really see,
> But how immense the difference,
>   It makes to you and me!

THE congregation had grown smaller and smaller during the wintry weather until the evening came when the vicar began the service with the customary words "Dearly beloved" — and she blushed!

SNOW RAPTURE

THE FRIENDSHIP BOOK

AN inscription at the church of St Stephen's Walbrook, in London, says, "O God, make the door of this house wide enough to receive all who need human love and fellowship".

When I read this I thought of a piece written by the late Dr W. E. Sangster, the Methodist preacher. He tells us that one Christmas Day, when he was in the Army, he felt very lonely. He had been to a church service and was walking back to the barracks in a murky drizzle.

Suddenly, out of the darkness, stepped a civilian. He had seen the doctor in church, and wondered if he would care to spend the rest of the day with his family.

Will Sangster was made very welcome. He sat by the fire and played with the children, experiencing the true meaning of the season.

This Christmas season, may we, too, "Make the door of our home wide enough to receive all who need human love and fellowship."

REACH UP!

I FEEL such joy when I see rising things:
A sunflower climbing up above a wall,
A purple mountain, or a pine tree tall;
A skylark starting on an upward flight,
A candle flame with heavenward-pointed light;
These natural things remind me to be wise.
They show that I should also try to rise
Above depression . . . discord . . . hate and strife,
And reach up to the worthwhile things of life!
                                        Joyce Frances Carpenter

THE FRIENDSHIP BOOK

IT'S all too tempting to say exactly what we're thinking, especially if we're maybe not in the very best of humour. However, silence can be a wise policy as this apt quotation suggests:

"One minute of keeping your mouth shut is worth an hour of explanation".

HANGING up stockings or pillowcases in Britain or putting out wooden sabots in The Netherlands — these are only two of the ways in which children prepare to receive their Christmas gifts.

There is an interesting custom, too, in parts of Germany where girls are given a rather special large ball of wool. As they start to knit, small gifts fall out — a ring, a coin, a brooch and so on — till they come to the centre where they find the best present of all.

I sometimes think the year is rather like that as we work our way through it. Each season has its special joys — Spring flowers, Summer sun and holidays, Autumn with ripening harvests and the glory of the changing colour of the leaves, then, right at the end, Winter with Christmas — the best season of all. And not just because of parties and presents, of course, but because it marks the gift of Jesus whose coming to this world changed our lives.

GLORY to God in the highest, and on earth peace, good will toward men.   Luke 2,14.

THE FRIENDSHIP BOOK

THE Clarke family were all set for Christmas Day. They were to have their dinner at home, and they had been looking forward to it for weeks. Then, by chance, they discovered that an elderly neighbour was to be spending the day alone. Well, they couldn't have that, so they decided to invite her to share their festivities. To be honest, they weren't all that enthusiastic about it, but, as Mrs Clarke put it, "We wouldn't enjoy ourselves knowing that Bella was all alone, so we thought we might as well."

It turned out to be the happiest Christmas Day possible! No one could remember more laughter, good cheer or so many beaming faces.

"It sounds strange," commented one of the family afterwards, "but we felt as if our home had been truly blessed."

The following year, the Clarkes didn't wait to find out if Bella was to be on her own — they issued an early invitation to make sure that she would be with them. And you won't be surprised to hear that she'll be with them this year, too . . .

HAVE you heard the story of the man in the jungle who came face to face with a tiger?

It was a terrifying experience — his bullets were all used up and he had nothing with which to defend himself. He sank to his knees and began to pray.

Suddenly he was aware that all was quiet. He opened his eyes and saw that the tiger was imitating him with its paws together and eyes closed.

He was beginning to feel secure again when the tiger opened one eye, and grinned, "I don't know what *you* said, but I've just been saying grace!"

DECEMBER TAPESTRY

THE FRIENDSHIP BOOK

WEDNESDAY—DECEMBER 27.

J UST after Christmas, an evening paper in County Cork published a small boy's letter:

"Dear Santa Claus — at Christmas I was given a sister instead of a bike. Maybe some other boy wanted a sister and received my bike. We have kept the sister but I'd still like a bike."

Another youngster was even more direct: "Dear Santa — you seemed to have trouble getting my tractor and bicycle last time. Have you tried the Yellow Pages?"

THURSDAY—DECEMBER 28.

T HE West Highland Railway, on its way to the sea at Mallaig, runs through some of the most glorious scenery in the world. Sections of it presented severe engineering problems and though it may be hard to believe, one of these was solved in a dentist's chair!

There was simply not enough power to operate all the drills needed to drive through the hard rock to make tunnels and cuttings. Young Malcolm MacAlpine, son of Robert MacAlpine who was building the line, noticed when he was having a tooth filled, that the dentist operated the drill by pressing a knob on the floor.

He asked how it worked and was told that the knob controlled a flow of high pressure water. This gave Malcolm an idea. Could water power be used to drive a turbine that would provide compressed air for the rock drills?

It was thought that it could, and eventually, young Malcolm's inspiration led to a method producing four times as much power as was available before.

And all because of a visit to the dentist!

THE FRIENDSHIP BOOK

CHRISTINA ROSSETTI, the 19th century poet, is probably best known to most of us by her two Christmas hymns, "In the Bleak Mid-winter" and "Love Came Down at Christmas". Here is a saying of hers which should bring us help and inspiration at any time of the year:

"Better by far that you should forget and smile than that you should remember and be sad."

LOUIS was a little blind boy in the French town of Coupvray at a time when there was a lot of unemployment. It is recorded that in Coupvray alone there were 72 men who were unable to find a job and had time on their hands.

Some of them helped Louis by scratching a deep groove in the pathway down which he loved to wander, so that he could push his stick along it and follow the winding route safely as it twisted its way to a pond where he loved to play. Others helped him to learn where he was by listening to the chimes of the church clock.

When he grew older, Louis Braille never forgot the kindness of those unemployed men. As they had helped him so he, too, assisted others by inventing the system of reading and writing which is still a blessing to blind people the world over.

NOW unto God and our Father be glory for ever and ever. Amen.   Philippians 4:20

Where The Photographs Were Taken

RYDAL WATER, CUMBRIA — *Winter Tracery.*

GLEN DOLL, ANGUS — *Nature's Glory.*

LULWORTH COVE, DORSET — *Escape.*

HUNGERFORD, BERKSHIRE — *Country Calm.*

RIVER KENNET, BERKSHIRE — *Precious Times.*

WORTH MATRAVERS, DORSET — *Legacy.*

DRUM CASTLE, ABERDEENSHIRE — *Surprise.*

BROADSANDS BAY, PAIGNTON — *Willing Hands.*

LOCH MORAR LODGE, INVERNESS-SHIRE —
Beneath Blue Skies.

MAN O' WAR BAY, DORSET — *Just Think.*

MONSALL DALE, DERBYSHIRE — *Bright Morning.*

SHERWOOD FOREST — *Admiration.*

LAKE OF MENTEITH, PERTHSHIRE — *Gratitude.*

BURNHAM BEECHES, BUCKINGHAMSHIRE —
Golden Moments.

TARN HOWS, CUMBRIA — *Snow Rapture.*

DERWENTWATER, CUMBRIA — *December Tapestry.*

Printed and Published by D. C. THOMSON & Co. Ltd.,
185 Fleet Street, London EC4A 2HS.

© D. C. Thomson & Co. Ltd., 1988.

ISBN 0 85116 433 1